Freestyle Canoeing
Contemporary Paddling Technique

Freestyle Canoeing
Contemporary Paddling Technique

by Lou Glaros and Charlie Wilson

MENASHA RIDGE PRESS
BIRMINGHAM, ALABAMA

Printed in the United States of America
Published by Menasha Ridge Press
First Edition, First Printing

Library of Congress Cataloging-in-Publication Data
Glaros, Lou, 1951-
    Freestyle canoeing: contemporary paddling technique/by Lou Glaros and Charile Wilson.
— 1st ed.
        p. cm.
    ISBN 0-89732-122-7 : $14.95
    1. Canoes and canoeing.   I. Wilson, Charlie, 1946-   .
    II. Title.
    GV783.G56   1994
    796.1'22—dc20
                                                            94-6934
                                                            CIP

Text design by Frank Logue
of Carolina Graphics Group

Menasha Ridge Press
3169 Cahaba Heights Road
Birmingham, Alabama 35243

Table of Contents

Acknowledgments

It's been some year—long hours bent over a word processor or madly redlining a first draft; marathon photo sessions followed by those indecisive hours of "picking just the right shots"; and the seemingly insurmountable task of coordinating a southeastern writer (Lou) and a midwestern one (Charlie). Was it worth it? We hope so, but any success is also due to incredible support received from friends and the entire canoe industry.

We'd like to express our gratitude to the Freestyle's formative leaders—Dave Curtis, Harold Deal, Mike Galt, Frank Hosford, Mickey Landry, Pat Moore, Harry Roberts, and Phil Sigglekow—for their early efforts, gentle tutelage, and continuing support.

We deeply appreciate the numerous canoe and paddle manufacturers who so generously loaned equipment for the photo shoots, so essential to this work. This includes Avant Canoe, Bell Canoe, Blackhawk Canoe, Curtis Canoe, Dagger Canoe and Paddles, Grey Owl Paddles, Ibis Paddles, Loon Works, Mad River Canoe, Mitchell Paddles, Patagonia, Quimby Paddles, Sawyer Canoe, Swift Canoe, We-No-Nah Canoe, and Wilderness Systems/ Lotus Canoe.

Mostly, though, we thank our Freestyle paddling friends and families—those unsung heroes who stuck by us while this work took shape—Debbie DeBerry, Ed DeBerry, Carol Glaros, Melissa Glaros, Mary Lou Greene, Dana Grover, Jude Habermann, Tom MacKenzie, Ellen Merrill, Pam Meyers, Mary Katherine Rountree, Eric Schooley, Doug Sphar, Deborah Welbes, Sam West, Chase Wilson, and Drake Wilson.

They advised us, reviewed our work, edited, helped with the word processing, encouraged us, photographed, and were photographed. It's hard work dressing to the nines, climbing into a canoe, and tooling around before three cameras while being criticized for technique, posture, hull placement, and bad hair. And then being asked to repeat that last maneuver again because a motor drive malfunctioned.

Thanks, people, it's great fun to work with creative friends who exhibit such grace under pressure.

Part I: The Preliminaries

Or "It's Best to Begin at the Beginning."

Introduction

FREESTYLE! The name conjures up flashy images: athletic young men and women swinging dangerously close to a ski boat, performing stunts over the wake; snow skiers dressed in neon colors flipping, twisting, and convoluting through aerial stunts; or carefree competitors crouched low over their skateboards, rocketing back and forth, up and down, across a high-banked track. Compelling visions, but not the ones we're after.

Freestyle—as in freestyle canoeing—is a genteel endeavor, more akin to free skating than to the examples above. Freestyle is sport paddling for quietwater, a discipline that emphasizes precise boat handling through graceful paddle control. As you become familiar with freestyle, you'll discover that it is not a power sport. Athletic actions are replaced by elegant, fluid movement. You'll find that it is based on familiar strokes and moves, modified with special enhancements, and that it's a technique for efficient paddling: useful on day trips, longer tours, and for "just messin' around."

Mostly, though, you'll find it to be a lifestyle activity with its own vocabulary, elegant equipment, and intensive physical skills. Freestyle paddling blends traditional canoeing skills with responsive new equipment and it meets our society's demand for excellence in recreational activity. Freestyle emphasizes elegant canoe control, becoming a non-intrusive mode of self expression on the water, and it meshes nicely with modern lifestyles. It is far easier to free thirty minutes at either end of a day than an entire weekend, and that half hour of paddling on the park pond can help us prepare for the day's onslaught or unwind afterwards.

Freestyle canoeing celebrates the beauty of motion on water. Most of us paddle not to win a medal or catch a fish or move to the next scenic campsite, but rather to enjoy the physical activity of paddling. It doesn't matter where

Freestyle canoeing celebrates the beauty of motion on water.

we paddle, but the more convenient the water, the better. We don't need to speed across great distances and we don't need stable, freight-carrying capacity because we generally don't paddle on violent water. We can use short, lightweight, responsive hulls—canoes that are user-friendly and fun to paddle. But it's the paddling that unleashes excitement.

Freestyle paddlers and their equipment come from a touring heritage, so sport hulls are typically designed to paddle efficiently and stay on course. To turn their pocket cruisers, freestyle paddlers lean the canoe to either rail. This lifts the stems and allows the boat to skid around a draw or pry in a variety of compelling maneuvers.

Freestyle is based on Canadian-style paddling. A fishing guide, kneeling against the bow seat with both knees tucked into the same chine, entertained his customers with fancy paddling at day's end. Those sixteen-foot Prospectors were fair-play boats when both stems were clear, and they eased the development of the onside moves we use today.

American Freestyle grew out of the interaction of Mike Galt's Dandy, a solo canoe designed in 1975, and Pat Moore's experience with Canadian-style paddling garnered during Olympic training north of the border. Pat mastered the onside moves and then Harold Deal introduced cross strokes and heels.

Freestyle's greatest risk is an unplanned swim in a friendly park lake.

There was interesting stuff going on—new maneuvers being developed and new equipment to do them in. New concepts in hull configuration developed. Paddle blades grew in size, better combining the functions of power, draw, and brace. Meanwhile, freestyle's greatest risk was, and still is, an unplanned swim in the friendly park lake.

At first, freestyle canoeing developed slowly until solo canoeing experienced a significant growth period in the early eighties. As a nation, we are a people driven by personal pursuits. We drive our own cars, figure our taxes on personal computers and unwind with individualized hobbies, so why not personal canoes? They have their advantages. Every paddler in control of his or her own destiny—what a compelling concept! When used for escape, introspection or wildlife appreciation, a solo canoe can't be beat. There are no discussions about which side of the island to run to or whether to stop and inspect a spider web.

But most individuals are gregarious, and therein lies the real beauty of solo canoeing. Solo paddlers are free to intermingle, free to pull abeam of someone for a short chat and then move on to play in a quiet pool or explore an interesting side stream. Solo paddling offers each individual the opportunity to combine social interaction with private solitude on the same day trip.

Freestyle followed closely on the heels of the solo paddling movement. It was a natural progression, as solo paddlers began searching for alternatives—for something more exciting than power paddling for mind-numbing miles. Above all, quietwater paddling is a skill-intensive sport, an activity that could be enjoyed at a higher level if it were practiced with studied grace and precision; an activity performed for its own benefits, not just to go somewhere, but to have fun—you know, *play*!

The practical application of freestyle technique is found when winding down tight, twisting streams, the kind of waterways that many paddlers negotiate either by ricocheting from bank to bank, or by playing bumper pool with every rock. The fluid rhythm of the practiced freestylist also allows incredibly close encounters with wildlife, a benefit greatly appreciated by the naturalist and birdwatcher inside each of us.

The skills that permit precise boat control on some winding little stream are the same skills that beg to be played with. And so it happens that the more ardent practitioners began experimenting with wild maneuvers. Soon a new vocabulary of moves emerged—axles, posts, wedges, christies, linked combinations—exhilarating maneuvers featuring bow-down skids, thrilling offside leans, and radical paddle placements.

Strangely, it was nearly a decade before the freestyle technique of 1980 migrated to tandem canoes. Tandem paddling is something everyone can identify with—whether they attended camp as a youth or learned by trial and error in a rental canoe at the local livery. Unlike solos, tandems have two paddlers who complement each other, one turns the leading end while the other powers the hull. Tandem maneuvers are faster than solo moves and offer an almost infinite variety of combinations.

The basics are learned faster in solo crafts, but the satisfaction of interactive teamwork—working in tandem, sharing synergistic actions—is rewarding and fun. This interaction can be compelling for either the novice paddler first experiencing the thrill of working in harmony with another or the practiced duo linking precise maneuvers while gracefully directing their boat down a tight stream. Sport tandem paddling has arrived with the nineties.

The basics are learned faster in solo crafts, but the satisfaction of interactive teamwork is rewarding and fun.

That arrival has brought greater profile to the sport of freestyle, along with increased interest and acceptance. Freestyle programs, instructional clinics, and competitions have sprung up around the country and have been featured at numerous national shows including the L.L. Bean North American Canoe Symposium, the Southwestern Canoe Rendezvous, and each Conclave held since 1987.

The American Canoe Association has formed a Freestyle Activity Committee which has developed solo and tandem freestyle technique workshops and criteria for freestyle instructor training. The word is also spreading through the written media. Canoeing books by Cliff Jacobson and Slim Ray include chapters on freestyle. *Canoe* magazine carries articles on freestyle, and *Paddler* magazine features regular columns on freestyle technique.

Sound interesting? Maybe freestyle paddling is for you. If so, read on, because that's what this book is all about—a complete source of information for any paddler wishing to learn freestyle technique. Is it a text book? Yeah, sort of, and it contains a chapter on the physics of paddling, one on hull design, and another on paddles. It's not highly technical, mind you, just enough detail to whet your appetite—only the fundamentals and how they relate to freestyle paddling—we promise, no equations.

Is it a reference book? Partly. A chapter on accessories presents information on the basic equipment required for an enjoyable trip on the water. Read about PFDs, knee blocks, and small packs to conveniently carry all the items you'll need. Do you need a refresher course on car topping your canoe or carrying it to the water? Then read the chapter on logistics.

Is it a training manual? We certainly hope so, because that's why we wrote it. There's a chapter on solo technique and another one on tandem, both subdivided into separate sections, each describing a particular stroke, maneuver, or linked combination. We've tried to sequence the descriptions in order of increasing difficulty and, in many cases, we mention a variety of alternatives. The sections contain numerous photographs displaying the maneuver in sequence and showing key features. In all cases, the photographs are numbered and listed where applicable in the text.

Bear in mind that this book has no connected plot and, although we'd like to think it makes for interesting and informative reading, we doubt if many readers will cruise through its pages, beginning to end. However, it does contain a wealth of information that any canoeist can sink teeth into; whether it's the maneuver descriptions, the technical reference chapters or the chapters that introduce freestyle competitions and games.

Grab your paddle, slide your canoe onto a mirror-smooth lake and "lay it on the rail."

So please read on and enjoy. If we've done our job, before long your copy of this book will be well-worn with dog-eared pages, a broken spine, and maybe even wrinkles from water spots. We're two average paddlers who stumbled into freestyle and fell madly in love with it. We want to instill that same excitement into your quietwater paddling. So grab your paddle, slide your canoe onto a mirror-smooth lake, and "lay it on the rail." We hope to meet you on the water someday.

Applied Physics
"Isaac Newton: Paddling Guru"

Picture this: In the not-so-distant past a young man was paddling at a lake near his home, practicing some of the exciting freestyle moves he had recently learned. On one particular pass he was really flying. He swept the boat around to the left, rolled the right rail into the water, and jammed his paddle against the gunwale in a "sort of" bow pry. "Woooaa!" SPLASH! Before he knew it, the boat slid out from under him and he simply fell in.

"What happened?" he asked himself as he surfaced and began pushing the canoe toward shore. Then it occurred to him, "It's really quite simple and obvious," he thought. "The hydrodynamic force on the paddle blade was acting below my center of rotation, creating a torque that pulled me in one direction and pushed the canoe in the other. Then...." But wait, this story is getting way ahead of itself. Consider this.

By vocation, the young man was an engineer and, by avocation, a paddler—two seemingly incongruous activities. But, not so. You see, engineering is nothing more than the understanding of how things work and then the application of that knowledge to make things work better. And doesn't it seem natural that if a paddler understands why a canoe does what it does—why it reacts a certain way to given paddle strokes—then that person can use that knowledge to become a more proficient paddler. There's a connection. Knowledge and understanding breed improvement. And that's what this narration is all about.

Knowledge and understanding breed improvement.

Perhaps this chapter should really begin in seventeenth century England with a young man named Isaac Newton. "Isaac Newton! Say, isn't he the fellow who invented gravity?" Well, not quite, that was done by a much higher authority. What Newton did, though, was simply(?) develop a theory that systematically explained the natural motion of objects, and until Albert Einstein rocked the world with the concept of relativity, Newton's three laws of motion were the bedrock of all classical mechanics. In fact, for the average person, they are still the foundation of most everyday actions (including paddling a canoe).

What, then, are these laws that so irrevocably govern our lives? Consider these statements from a standard college physics book:

1. First Law—a body will remain at rest or in constant motion until it is acted upon by an outside force.
2. Second Law—the greater the force on a body, the greater its acceleration will be.
3. Third Law—for every action there is an equal and opposite reaction.

Interesting, but how does it apply to paddling a canoe? Well, let's examine it a piece at a time and see how it all ties together.

It's fairly well known that there are three major forces that act on a canoe. First, there is the hydrodynamic force that the surrounding water exerts on the boat hull. This includes buoyancy, which lifts the boat and counteracts the weight of the canoe, resisting the tendency to sink (sure sounds like a nice feature). It also includes water resistance—the drag force, due to friction between the hull and water, which tends to slow the boat down (not so good, huh?).

Secondly, consider the wind. Almost everyone who has paddled in open water in windy conditions will attest to the fact that it can exert a sizable aerodynamic force. In effect, the wind strikes the exposed "sail" area of the canoe and pushes it along. Headwinds are certainly troublesome. They resist our forward motion and make us paddle harder to maintain speed. Contrary to popular beliefs, tailwinds are not always welcomed companions. Sure, they push us in the direction we are paddling, but just like sidewinds, they may also induce undesirable rotations, causing us to exert additional forces to control the direction of the canoe.

The most important force a boater should understand is the control force applied by the paddle.

Undoubtedly the most important force a boater should understand, though, is the control force applied by the paddle. With it we thrust the canoe forward or selectively slow it down. We change the direction the boat is pointing or simply sideslip without rotating. It can even be used to brace us from falling into the water, or conversely, as any freestyle paddler/engineer has witnessed countless times, it can forcibly eject us from the canoe—definitely a force worth understanding.

Had Isaac Newton been a paddler he would have instantly understood how a paddle is used to create a force. He might have reasoned it out in the following manner. First he'd have drawn a picture much like the one shown in Figure 1, which depicts a canoe sitting motionless in the water and a paddle

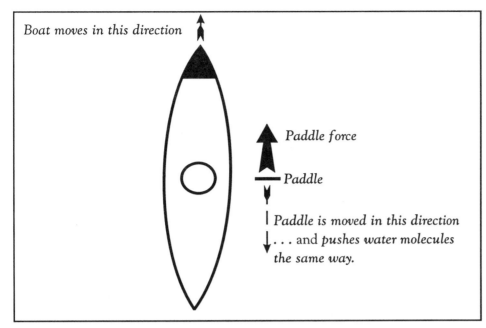

Boat moves in this direction

Paddle force

Paddle

Paddle is moved in this direction
*. . . and pushes water molecules
the same way.*

*Figure 1: Anatomy of a
Forward Stroke.*

being pulled through the water toward the stern. The dashed arrow represents the direction the paddle is being moved. It also represents the direction that the paddle is "pushing" the nearby water molecules.

At this point, young Newton might have jumped up and exclaimed, "Ah hah! I understand! This is a clear application of my third law of motion. If my paddle pushes the water in the direction shown, then undoubtedly, the water must push back (react) on my paddle in the opposite direction. He would then have drawn the bold arrow entitled the "paddle force."

"Now," Newton continues, "because my canoe was originally at rest and I just applied a paddle force to it, then, according to my first law of motion, it will begin moving in the direction of the force. If I want it to accelerate, all I have to do is increase the force by pushing harder against the water. That's my second law in action."

Of course, Newton's logic would work regardless of the direction that the paddle is moved. This why the draw and pry strokes pull and push a canoe sideways (Figures 2 and 3) and why diagonal strokes (Figure 4) will move the boat at other angles.

Simple, huh? The boat moves in the direction of the force applied to it and the force is opposite to the direction that the paddle is moved. Right? Well, not quite. You see, according to the third law of motion, the force is opposite to the direction that the nearby water molecules are pushed and that may be different from the motion of the paddle.

For instance, suppose the paddle is pulled through the water while the face of the blade makes an angle with the direction of motion. As shown in Figure 5, this angle is called the pitch angle (aeronautical engineers call it the angle of attack), and because of it, the blade acts like an airplane wing and pushes the water in the direction shown by the dotted line.

The force is opposite to the direction that the nearby water molecules are pushed and that may be different from the motion of the paddle.

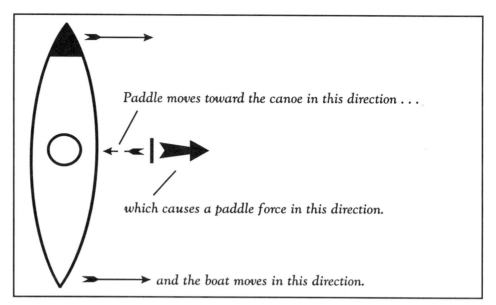

Paddle moves toward the canoe in this direction . . .

which causes a paddle force in this direction.

and the boat moves in this direction.

Figure 2: The Draw Stroke.

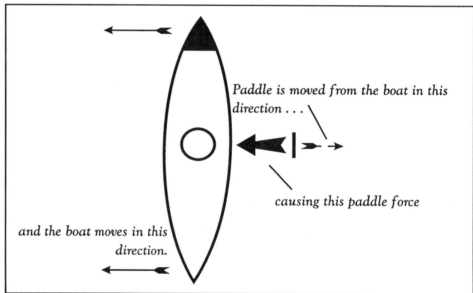

Paddle is moved from the boat in this direction . . .

causing this paddle force

and the boat moves in this direction.

Figure 3: The Pry Stroke.

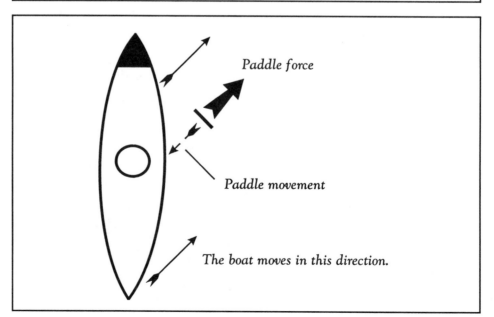

Paddle force

Paddle movement

The boat moves in this direction.

Figure 4: A "Diagonal" Stroke.

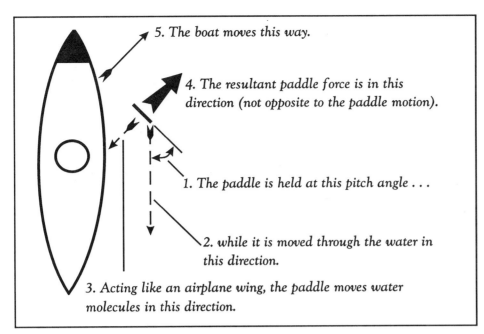

Figure 5: A More General Stroke.

1. The paddle is held at this pitch angle . . .

2. while it is moved through the water in this direction.

3. Acting like an airplane wing, the paddle moves water molecules in this direction.

4. The resultant paddle force is in this direction (not opposite to the paddle motion).

5. The boat moves this way.

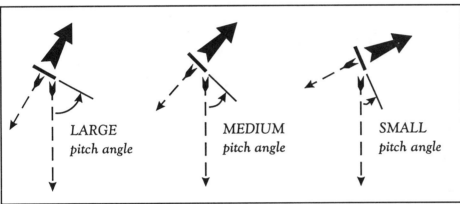

Figure 6: Pitch Angle Controls the Direction of Paddle Force.

LARGE *pitch angle*

MEDIUM *pitch angle*

SMALL *pitch angle*

Interestingly, this is almost the same as striking a tennis ball with a tennis racquet. If you hold the racquet perpendicular to the direction you are swinging, then the ball will be pushed in that same direction. But, if you hold the racquet at an angle, the ball will fly off in a different, but predictable, direction.

So if the pitch angle of a paddle is changed, then the direction the water molecules are moved is also changed (Figure 6); therefore, altering the pitch angle becomes a primary method for modifying the direction of the paddle force.

Neat, huh? But certainly not revolutionary. In fact, if you can do a sculling stroke, then you're already familiar with the concept (if not in theory, at least in effect). During a sculling stroke, the paddle is sliced back and forth through the water parallel to the keelline of the canoe. The pitch angle is held such that the resultant paddle force is always in the same direction (perpendicular to the keelline).

This is illustrated in Figure 7, which demonstrates a sculling draw stroke. Note that during the first half of this motion, shown in Figure 7 (part I), the

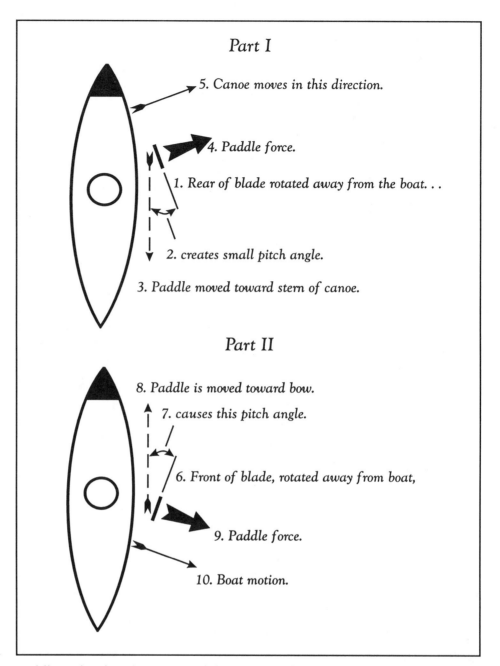

Part I

5. Canoe moves in this direction.

4. Paddle force.

1. Rear of blade rotated away from the boat. . .

2. creates small pitch angle.

3. Paddle moved toward stern of canoe.

Part II

8. Paddle is moved toward bow.

7. causes this pitch angle.

6. Front of blade, rotated away from boat,

9. Paddle force.

10. Boat motion.

Figure 7: The Sculling Draw.

paddle is sliced to the stern and the pitch angle is created by first rotating the rear of the blade away from the boat. By Newton's laws, the resultant force pulls the boat to the right.

For the second half of the stroke (part II), the paddle is first turned so the front edge is away from the canoe. When the paddle is sliced forward, the applied force again pulls the boat to the right. Make sense? Try drawing a similar set of diagrams for the sculling pry stroke and see if the concept becomes clearer.

Well, by now young Newton must have been ecstatic because he realized that by pushing, pulling, or slicing a paddle through the water he could create a force that would move a stationary canoe. But, then, like all great scientists (and budding canoeists), Isaac made that next great leap forward when he

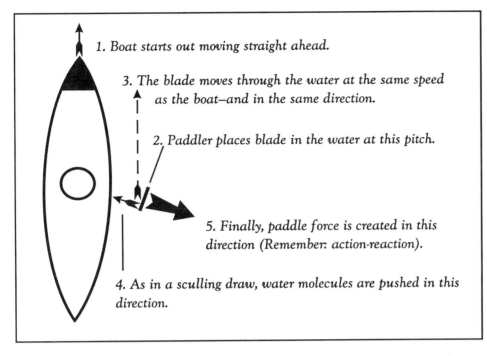

1. Boat starts out moving straight ahead.

3. The blade moves through the water at the same speed as the boat—and in the same direction.

2. Paddler places blade in the water at this pitch.

5. Finally, paddle force is created in this direction (Remember: action-reaction).

4. As in a sculling draw, water molecules are pushed in this direction.

Figure 8: Anatomy of a Moving Stroke.

recognized that he could also create a force in a moving canoe by just placing the paddle into the water and holding it at some pitch angle.

As shown in Figure 8, he doesn't even have to move the paddle relative to the boat—he simply lets the motion of the canoe move the paddle through the water, pushing the nearby molecules in one direction to create a force in the opposite direction. BINGO! In one fell swoop, Newton has discovered a whole new set of strokes—the running draw and pry, the low and high brace, the hanging strokes, the static axles and posts, etc.—strokes that modern paddlers now take for granted.

Above all else, Newton was a keen observer of nature and a profound thinker always searching for answers to things he did not understand. So we might imagine the following scene unfolding as he discovers the "secret" of maneuvering a canoe. Isaac is at his local pond, paddling his favorite solo canoe. He is slowly getting angry. He can't keep the boat straight. Sure, every time he makes a forward stroke the canoe moves ahead, but damn, it also veers to the left!

Unable to contain his frustration any longer, he drives the boat ashore, hops out and stomps to the base of a large apple tree where he sits down to sulk. He picks up a bright red apple which just fell from the tree, missing his head by inches, and begins thinking about his dilemma. As he slowly devours the tasty fruit his gaze wanders to a pair of young children playing on a teeter totter in a park across the pond.

Instantly his mind clicks. "Of course!" he exclaims. "That's it. The canoe turns for the same reason the teeter totter rocks back and forth—because a force is applied at some distance from the pivot point (or center of rotation)."

"Thus," he continues, "when one of the kids sits at the end of the see-saw

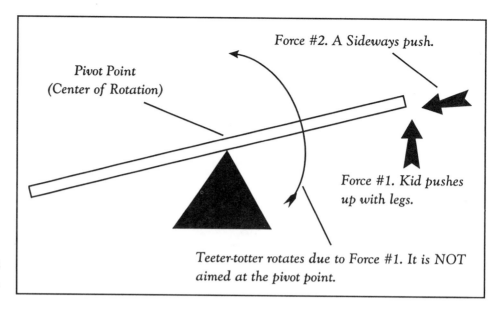

Figure 9: Turning a Teeter-Totter.

When the boater reaches out to perform a stroke, his paddle, arms, and body become the board of the teeter-totter.

and pushes up with his legs (Force #1 in Figure 9) the see-saw rotates. Conversely, if the kid had been standing behind the teeter totter and had pushed along the length of the board toward the pivot point (that's Force #2, now), the thing would not have turned." Which leads to Isaac's key discovery—the see-saw *will* turn when the applied force (a push, pull, or whatever) is not directed at its center of rotation and it *will not* turn if the force is pointed at its center of rotation.

Similarly, the same truth holds for a canoe (Figure 10). In the case of the solo canoe, the middle of the boat, where the pivot point is (under most conditions), also happens to be close to the paddler's location. When the boater reaches out to perform a stroke, his paddle, arms, and body become the board of the teeter totter (You know, the hand bone's connected to wrist bone, the wrist bone's connected to the arm bone, and so on). So when he does a forward stroke, the resultant paddle force (Force #1 in Figure 10) pushes forward against the blade but, because the force is not directed through the pivot point, the canoe turns to the left; the offside.

When the solo canoeist does a pry stroke and pushes the paddle directly away from himself, the resultant force (Force #2) is aimed right at him (the pivot point). Therefore, even though the boat will move to the left, it *will not* turn. Interestingly, if the paddler had placed the blade in the water closer to the stern and then did the pry stroke (Figure 11), the paddle force would not be directed towards him and, *voila*, the boat would turn to the right, his onside. Just like the teeter totter.

"Holy Liverpool," shouts Isaac as he leaps up and runs to his canoe, "I've gotta try this!" He grabs his paddle and pushes off. He then spends the remainder of the afternoon playing—trying all the strokes he can think of and observing how the canoe responds. In every case, the boat does exactly as he expected. His theory worked!

Unfortunately, he still had not solved his original dilemma—he still

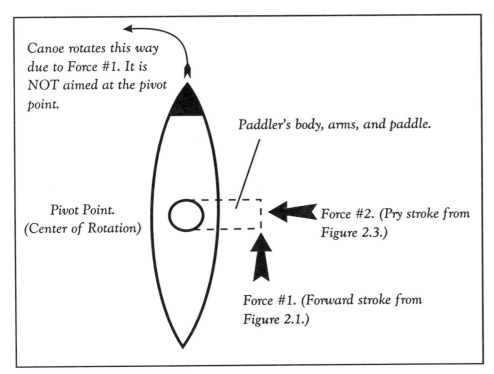

Canoe rotates this way due to Force #1. It is NOT aimed at the pivot point.

Paddler's body, arms, and paddle.

Pivot Point. (Center of Rotation)

Force #2. (Pry stroke from Figure 2.3.)

Force #1. (Forward stroke from Figure 2.1.)

Figure 10: Turning a Canoe.

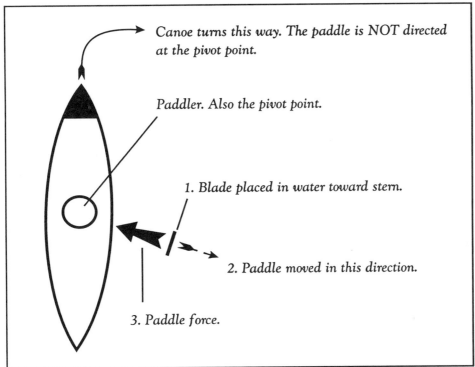

Canoe turns this way. The paddle is NOT directed at the pivot point.

Paddler. Also the pivot point.

1. Blade placed in water toward stern.

2. Paddle moved in this direction.

3. Paddle force.

Figure 11: The Stern Pry.

couldn't go straight. Sure, he knew exactly what to do with his paddle to turn the canoe any direction he wanted, but just try and go straight—his theory didn't provide an adequate solution to that problem.

He even went so far as to invent the forward stroke shown in Figure 12 (From Newton's lab notes, under the working title of *Prolegemena to a Preliminary Discussion of Introductory Thoughts on the Motion of the Common Canoe*). No doubt about it, the boat did move ahead, and because the force was aimed directly through his pivot point, it didn't turn. It didn't

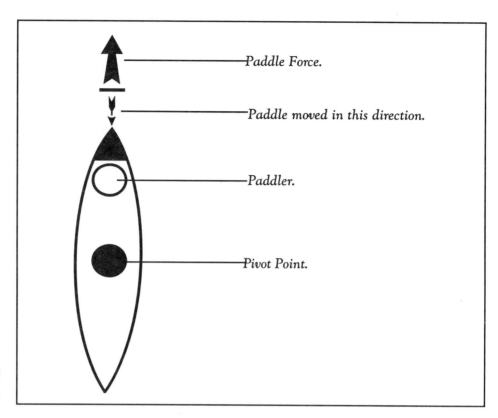

Paddle Force.

Paddle moved in this direction.

Paddler.

Pivot Point.

Figure 12: An Inefficient Forward Stroke.

take him long, though, to figure out that this stroke wasn't very efficient (seeing as how the paddler had to crawl forward and then extend over the bow just to make the correct motion).

"No!" Isaac said. "There just doesn't seem to be a single stroke that will work."

And then, in one of his recurring flashes of brilliance, young Newton realized what he had said and how it answered his puzzling dilemma.

"Of course, a single stroke can't do the job," he thought, "but how about a number of separate strokes pieced together? Each one would cause the canoe to move and turn differently, but when the whole sequence was completed, the boat would be moving forward and would be pointed in the correct direction."

So, he began experimenting, trying various combinations of strokes. Finally, he hit upon one that seemed to work and he quickly drew it on a piece of scratch paper he had in his pocket. (A copy of this historical work is shown in Figure 13.)

He reasoned that if he first did a draw stroke aimed at the bow of the canoe, the canoe would turn to the inside (the right) because the paddle force would not be in line with the pivot point. Okay, if he now quickly turns the paddle counterclockwise and pulls it back through the water, the boat is propelled forward, but for the reasons discussed earlier, it also veers to the offside (the left), overshooting the direction the boat was originally pointed.

In order to "correct" for the overshoot, he turns the paddle further counterclockwise and performs a stroke directed away from the stern.

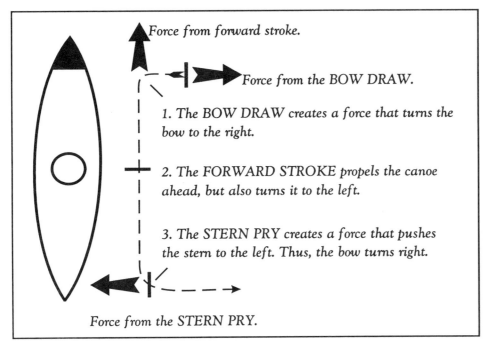

Force from forward stroke.

Force from the BOW DRAW.

1. The BOW DRAW creates a force that turns the bow to the right.

2. The FORWARD STROKE propels the canoe ahead, but also turns it to the left.

3. The STERN PRY creates a force that pushes the stern to the left. Thus, the bow turns right.

Force from the STERN PRY.

Figure 13

Naturally, the resultant force also does not act through the pivot point. Therefore, the canoe rotates back to the onside. NEAT! Now, the boat has moved ahead and is pointed in the original direction. Exactly what Isaac wanted to do.

Of course, Newton could sense that even this stroke sequence was somewhat inefficient. After all, during two segments of the motion (the bow draw and the stern correction), the forces aren't even aimed forward and, so, don't apply any propulsion. After a little thought, though, Newton decided that maybe this inefficiency could be corrected by simply smoothing out the sequence of moves so that it was not quite so square. So he tried it, and sure enough, the resultant motion was much more pleasant.

Before he forgot what he had done, he quickly traced his new stroke on the back of his scratch paper (Figure 14). He held it up at arms length and looked at it. He was proud of what he had discovered. He was very proud. He had finally seen the answer to the problem that had plagued his paddling for so long. "I see," he said, "I finally see!" (Note: Some historians contend that this is the origin of the name "SEE" stroke. Or is that "C" stroke?)

Well, enough of this historical fantasy. Even young Newton's gullible Uncle Fig wouldn't believe it. But maybe, just maybe, it will serve to illustrate how natural paddling a canoe really is. There is one well-known canoe designer who compares paddling with treading water. What? That's right. The hand motions we use to control the orientation of our bodies while in the water are instinctive, and while in a canoe, the paddle is really just an extension of our hands. We instinctively create forces that do not act through our pivot points, so we turn. It's just natural that this should also apply to paddling skills.

Now, do you remember that "sort of" bow pry mentioned at the start of

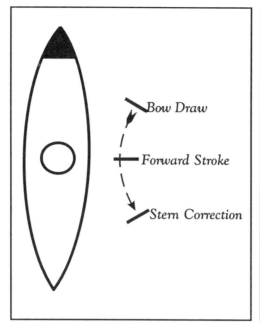

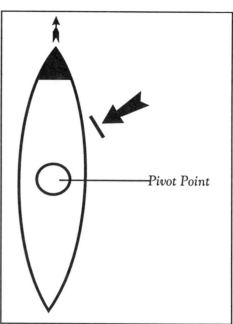

Figure 14(at left): The "Smoothed-Out" Forward Stroke (The Infamous C-Stroke).

Figure 15(at right): The Bow Wedge.

Canoes are not mystical creations . . . they react to external forces the way any everyday object does.

this chapter? Yeah, that's right, the one that pitched our intrepid freestyle paddler out of the canoe. Well, that "bow wedge," a heeled maneuver using a bow jam, follows the same rules we've been discussing. As the boat is moving forward, the paddle is placed in the water next to the canoe at the angle shown in Figure 15. The nearby water molecules are pushed away from the boat and the resultant force acts in the opposite direction—towards the bow! BINGO, the canoe rotates to the offside (the left); as desired.

But, why did he fall in? Was he pushed in? Did he lose his balance? Well yeah, sort of. On both counts. To understand why, you have to see what the stroke looks like from directly in front of the boat (Figure 16). Clearly, the same paddle force that pushes on the bow in front of the pivot point also pushes on the hull below the pivot point. The result? The boat is rotated out from under our paddler and he simply falls in.

Of course, there's more to it than that, and every time you do a jam stroke it's not a foregone conclusion that you're going to swim. But the tendency is there, and you should be prepared. In fact, by understanding the forces that are trying to pitch you from the boat, you can develop techniques that will counteract those tendencies.

And maybe that's the point of this whole chapter. Canoes are not mystical creations that are governed by magical incantations and spells. They react to external forces the way any everyday object does. If you pull on them or push on them, they move and rotate in a very predictable manner. And that holds true whether the external force is applied by a paddle, the slap of a breaking wave against the hull, or the push of a stiff crosswind against the exposed "sail" area. It holds true for solo canoes as well as tandem canoes, and for novice paddlers as well as experts. The results are always the same.

So, now consider our budding freestylist paddling with several friends at a

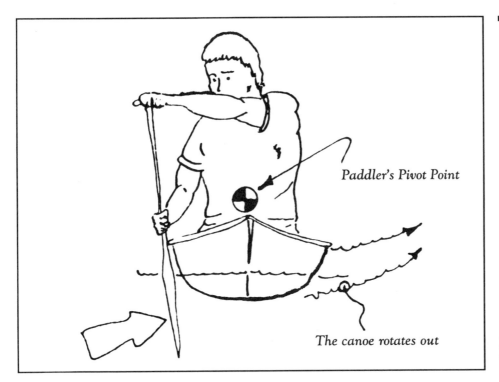

Paddler's Pivot Point

The canoe rotates out

Figure 16: Why the Bow Wedge Might Throw You.

lake near his home and practicing some new moves and strokes. On one particular pass he was really flying. He did an exaggerated correction at the end of a C stroke, laid the paddle out diagonally behind the canoe, shifted his weight toward the bow and rolled the right rail into the water at the same time. As the hull was pushed into the turn, he reached forward and pulled a dramatic bow draw under the boat. When the sequence was finished, the canoe had turned completely around and was moving in the opposite direction.

"Wow," said one of his co-horts, who had witnessed the whole thing, "that was really nice."

"Thanks." he replied, "I learned it from a fellow named Newton."

Hull Shape, Construction, and Selection

Freestyle canoes are personal boats reflecting the size, paddling style, and personality of their owners. Shorter, narrower, and lighter than other canoes, they lack the speed of longer hulls, but by virtue of slender shaping, they feature greater energy efficiency. And they are responsive! It's an interesting combination. Freestyle canoes must offer speed and tracking ability while maintaining maneuverability. How do you select a boat meeting these contradictory requirements?

Size

A personal canoe must be small and light enough to encourage use. If you can't pick up your boat easily or place it in car racks or carry it to the water's edge, you won't use it often. It's handy that smaller hulls, fitting smaller people, weigh less. Technologies that yield lighter canoes are expensive, but select the lightest canoe you can afford. You're the one who'll be carrying it, and none of us is getting younger. You'll paddle a canoe more if it's easy to carry and load.

If you can't pick up your boat easily you won't use it often.

Hull width should match the paddler's shoulder spread, and be narrow enough to allow unrestricted paddle motion on cross strokes. This is true for both solo and tandem canoes, but how narrow is narrow enough? That depends on you, the paddler.

First, the hull should be slender enough to allow your lower hand to hang at a comfortable angle under average paddling conditions. If you must lift your hand outward during a stroke to avoid hitting the gunwale, then the hull is too wide for comfortable or efficient paddling. Second, the hull must be narrow enough for you to work the paddle comfortably during a cross stroke. Finally, when the canoe is leaned in one direction, you must be able to reach over the high side to plant the paddle.

Under most conditions, longer canoes are faster than shorter canoes, but shorter canoes are easier to paddle. Shorter hulls have reduced surface area, resulting in lower skin friction, while longer hulls are more streamlined and produce less wave drag. Shorter canoes turn more easily while longer hulls keep course with less correction. Optimal length depends on loaded weight, paddler strength, tripping distance, and the selected tradeoff between turning and tracking.

Freestyle is often non-destinational and emphasizes wild turning techniques, so shorter canoes are dictated. Besides, smaller hulls are lighter—easier to carry and load in vehicles. Freestyle canoes range from twelve to fifteen feet in length for solos; from fourteen to sixteen feet for tandem craft.

Hull Shape

Most freestyle canoes are symmetrical. This means that, viewed from above, the hull is widest at its center with equal shaping toward both stems. Touring canoes are often asymmetrical, widest aft of center. This creates a more gently faired shape toward the bow resulting in greater forward efficiency. However, the long slender bows may lack adequate flotation, becoming unseaworthy in rough water and responding poorly to bow draws.

Hulls are occasionally reversely asymmetrical, widest forward of center. These "Cod-Head" designs provide an efficient but slow cruising speed, and with plenty of volume forward, they are quite seaworthy. Asymmetrical hulls can be tricky to handle, lengthening the paddler's learning curve. This is especially true for reverse maneuvers.

Freestyle canoes need to track efficiently . . . and turn quickly.

Rocker is best seen in side view as upturn of the keelline near bow or stern. Increased rocker reduces turning resistance—improved maneuverability at the expense of tracking control. Freestyle canoes need to track efficiently and so generally exhibit less than three inches of rocker. But they also need to turn quickly and for this purpose they are designed to be leaned securely to either side. This "heeling" creates instant rocker by lifting bow and stern upwards, which reduces turning resistance. Freestyle's graceful turns are enhanced by leaning the canoe to either side.

Cross-sectional shaping affects the stability and heeling effectiveness of the canoe. Of special interest are the chines, the area where the bottom of the canoe transitions into the sidewalls. Flat-bottomed canoes with vertical sides generally have abrupt chines that create instability when the boat is heeled. Freestyle canoes should possess gentle, broadly radiused chines that increase heeling predictability. Early freestyle canoes featured flared cross-sections. Coupled with a gentle chine, these hulls firmed up nicely when heeled to the rail.

Flared hulls are particularly user-friendly except that the paddler's shaft hand may intersect the hull. This is both uncomfortable and inefficient,

Photo 1: Compare a softly rounded hull with tumblehome to one with a hard chine and flare.

limiting the under-boat effect of the C stroke. Tumblehome, the inward curve of a flared hull, solves this problem. The bubble-sided shape has the secondary benefit of locating the rails closer together, allowing the hull to be heeled farther and lifting the stems higher for faster turns. On the down side, hulls with tumblehome have less volume at the rails and become finicky when the rail approaches water (Photo 1).

Some recent freestyle designs exhibit shouldered tumblehome, which carry the flare through a recurved tuck to an inset rail. The upper hull is narrow, offering lower hand clearance and increased heel angles while retaining the stability and dryness of constant flared designs. The disadvantage of shouldered designs is cost; constructed in multiple piece molds, they require more mold preparation and lamination time.

Construction and Materials

Freestyle hulls should have minimal weight and precise hull shaping. Thus, they are usually constructed of wood, wood and fabric, or plastic resin reinforced with fiberglass, Kevlar, carbon, or Spectra. No other materials available combine acceptable weight with the ability to retain compound shaping. While these constructions require hands-on techniques and are relatively expensive, they seem acceptable for a personal watercraft. And trim choices have a strong impact on finished product price.

Canoe trim—the rails, thwarts, end caps, and seating used to finish a canoe hull—is generally constructed of vinyl, extruded aluminum, or wood. While vinyl and aluminum components have their place in hulls abandoned to constant exposure to the elements, wood trim is favored by owners who appreciate its warmth, comfort, and beauty. Ash with an oiled finish is the industry standard. Furniture grade woods like cherry and walnut, varnished finishes, and custom shaping are considered deluxe treatment.

Almost everybody loves wood trim. It is beautiful, warm to the touch, and provides a tie to the days when all canoes were constructed of hand-fitted

Wood trim is favored by owners who appreciate its warmth, comfort, and beauty.

wood, but it requires care. Oiled trim should be reworked monthly; varnished trim requires more effort every few years. If you most store your canoe in the elements, consider your maintenance quotient when selecting wood.

Seating

Seats are an integral part of any canoe design and should be considered carefully. The seat not only supports the paddler's weight but also affects the control and forward efficiency of the canoe. The industry standard is an angled, flat cane bench pressed into an ash frame, but many other options are available.

Beginning paddlers often prefer bucket seats fitted low in the canoe. It's a viable seating arrangement and is ideal for cruising. The paddler's weight is centered and low, and in a large hull with camping gear, this can be quite stable. The paddler sits firmly in the bucket and is braced against lateral and rearward movement. A foot brace is mandatory, counteracting the tendency of forward strokes to pull the paddler forward and out of the seat.

But paddlers are not interested solely in cruising efficiency. Maneuverability may also be a premium and this is achieved by leaning the canoe. Sitting in a bucket seat with legs extended forward is not an ideal position for heeling a canoe. The best way to heel with security is to kneel with the legs spread wide. Here we recognize the need for a sufficient hull width to locate the knees comfortably yet with a stable stance in each chine.

The best way to heel with security is to kneel with the legs spread wide.

Pedestal seats offer a degree of control unavailable with other freestyle seating options. Properly fitted pedestals spread the paddler's knees into the chines and provide weight support through contact with the inner thighs. They add security for developing paddlers—the pedestal, gripped between both knees, can be swung back under the paddler with a hip snap should he or she lose control while heeling. The pedestal's disadvantage is its rigidity of seating position. Paddlers cannot slip both knees into one bilge in the comfortable and stable Canadian-style position. They cannot shift their weight forward or use the elegant high kneel position and often cannot slip their legs forward into a seated cruising stance. That lack of seating variation severely limits comfort and paddling options.

Most freestyle paddlers eventually gravitate to a bench seat with a gently radiused front edge that is comfortable to lean against. Slung high in the hull to provide adequate foot clearance, the seat should be positioned so the paddler's knees fall comfortably into the chines. Ideally, the bulk of the paddler's weight is borne by the front portion of the seat, and the knees are weighted just enough to be effective in heeling the canoe. From this position the legs can be easily shifted into other paddling positions. A sliding seat is a deluxe fixture permitting convenient fore and aft trim changes.

Tandems offer less seating variation than solo canoes—buckets or cane

Photo 2: Pedestal and cane seats.

benches are the only available options. They should be slung high for comfortable kneeling, although most boats are delivered from the manufacturer with seating mounted low to enhance perceived stability. Consider raising a seat if it's too low for comfortable kneeling. Seats should be angled forward for kneeling comfort, and ideally, the leading edge should be gently rounded to spread pressure over all of the paddler's backside. It is important that one tandem seat be adjustable because trim must be maintained regardless of the differential between bow and stern paddler weights. Many tandems provide an optional sliding bow seat. Trimable stern seating is rarely available.

A final seating problem concerns combination canoes, freestyle crafts that serve as solo boats and compact tandems. These canoes often come with cane or bucket seating in the bow and stern positions and a kneeling thwart for occasional solo use. The kneeling thwart is a well-shaped member that is mounted about one foot aft of the canoe's center. It is as comfortable as any other seat and requires less maintenance (Photo 2).

Knee Pads and Blocks

Knee pads and blocks improve comfort and heel control. They are a necessity in tandem bows where the narrowing hull forces the paddler's knees together. Thigh straps, favored by whitewater paddlers for the same function, limit the paddler's ability to move around comfortably in the canoes. They are generally ignored by quietwater enthusiasts.

Closed-cell foam pads are an inexpensive beginning, but they deteriorate and pick up irritating grit. Fabric coverings extend pad life and creature comfort and allow sand to be brushed off. Either way, the pad should grip both paddler and canoe securely, even when damp with bilge water, so test them wet.

The pad should grip both paddler and canoe securely, even when damp, so test them wet.

Stiff, closed-cell foam cups or wedges are often glued into sport canoes to improve fit and control. They are particularly useful in broadening the bow paddler's stance and in fitting relatively wide canoes to relatively short-legged paddlers. Cups are fine for a custom fit and offer the option of lifting with the high side knee during extreme heels, but wedges fit a wider range of people. Both are glued into canoes with contact cement. Test block location with the canoe in the water, then mark, measure, and remark before cleaning, drying, and gluing. Placing the cup straight up off a knee with the torso erect puts the rail near the water. Work done with contact cement is not easily undone and may compromise your canoe's value.

Paddles

She was a grand lady, graying hair pulled into a ponytail, intelligent eyes crowsfooting in a warm, glowing face. Over morning coffee at a weekend clinic on Lake Wisconsin, she was questioning us about the merits of various sport solo canoes.

Several cups of mud and a few flapjacks later, she'd determined to paddle them all, ordering a white Kev version of the one fitting her best. Strolling toward the freestyle beach, she took a detour towards a new, white, 7 series BMW. "I'll just get my paddle." Rummaging through the trunk, she emerged with a long Muskrat Made paddle. It had copper wire wrapped through holes that ran along both sides of an eight-inch split. The supposed waterfowl and sunset that ornamented the backface were indescribable. What was wrong?

The paddle, that stick in your hands, is the primary canoeing implement. An extra fifty dollars invested in a paddle has more impact on your equipage than an extra five hundred dollars invested in a hull. Here was an intelligent human being, driving a seventy-thousand-dollar car and purchasing her fourth two-thousand-dollar canoe, puttering around with a piece of kindling more suited to stirring paint than propelling a canoe.

An extra fifty dollars invested in a paddle has more impact than an extra five hundred dollars invested in a hull.

We dug through our paddle bags, loaning her a couple of workably sized sticks. When she drove home, she had a new canoe on order, three new paddles in the trunk, and a wry smile on her face.

She'd made a quantum leap as a paddler by beginning to use gear that enhanced her enjoyment of the sport.

The paddle controls the canoe's movement. The freestyle blade is fairly large in order to resist movement as we pull the hull towards the paddle and to provide enough bracing area at comfortable stroke cadences.

Paddle Blade Shape

Modern paddle width varies from eight and one-half inches to nine and one-half inches. Wider blades force the paddler farther over the canoe rail, narrower blades require inordinate length to catch enough water. Blade length varies from twenty-one to twenty-four inches on our multiple tracing; the shorter lengths are multiple-use production paddles, those over twenty-four inches are generally custom built for powerful paddlers.

Blade surface must match the individual paddler's size, strength, conditioning, and cadence. Larger blades transmit more power to the water through increased resistance to blade movement. This translates to greater acceleration, faster turns, more secure braces, and greater stress loading on various body parts. Freestyle's slower cadences limit stress, but the paddle that provides forward power and secure braces at thirty strokes a minute stresses the paddler at a cruising cadence. Use a smaller blade when it's time to move out.

Blades are subtly shaped to perform efficiently. A proper blade needs sloped, or relieved, shoulders, allowing the blade to pass under the canoe during the center portion of a forward stroke. Full shoulders keep the paddle farther abeam the keel. The bottom should be somewhat rounded; a radius of five to eight inches, with tighter radii, roughly two inches, in the corners. This tip shaping allows sure and quiet entry and exit from the water and reduces riffle chewing.

In summary, the freestyle blade should be about nine inches wide and about twenty-three inches long with additions or subtraction to fit paddler strength. Tapered shoulders and rounded ends reduce the surface area of our ideal paddle to about 160 square inches, plus or minus 20 square inches. Concerned about stressing joints? Select a smaller blade, providing more fluid shock absorption.

Cross-Sectional Shaping

Cross-sectional shaping is critical to elegant, effective slicing.

Freestyle paddlers often slice the paddle edgeways through the water in feathered maneuvers which combine bracing security with subtle drawing pressure and can be used for in-water recoveries. Cross-sectional shaping is critical to elegant, effective slicing. Blade edges don't have to cut bread, but finer ones allow the blade to slice with less resistance, turbulence, and flutter. More functional paddles feature fine edging with straight-line taper to the center rib.

Blades are longitudinally stiffened with ribs, reducing flex. Particularly on bent paddles, this rib is placed solely on the blade's backface. This is adequate for cruising but dysfunctional for sliced movement. The spine creates turbulence when water flows across it, increasing drag and deflecting the path of an imbalanced blade. Paddles that slice true need a blade with equal reinforcing on both faces to balance hydraulic jump, and both ribs should be

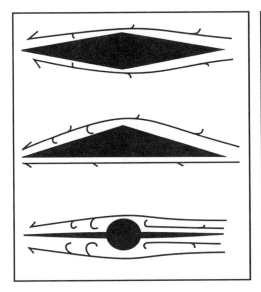

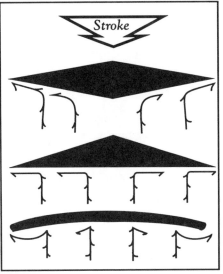

Figure 17 (at left): Slicing

Figure 18 (at right): Powerface Slip

well faired or blended in. Such blades are said to have balanced camber with dihedraled faces (Figure 17).

Recent research shows that cupped and flat power faces transmit more propulsive power, holding water on the face longer than cambered blades. The convex, dihedraled face allows water to stream off the paddle throughout the stroke where the flat and cupped faces lose purchase on water abruptly at the stroke's end. This is apparent in use, as cambered powerfaces ventilate easily. This is observable by watching the air drawn down the blade and off its edges when a partial vacuum is created by the water flowing off the blade. Cupped and flat powerfaces lose their catch on the water and ventilate suddenly with a glop and a shimmy. Emphasizing control rather than propulsive efficiency, a double-cambered blade is preferable for freestyle paddling (Figure 18).

Evaluate blade section using a dock. Stand pierside, knifing the paddle through the water, parallel to the dock edge. Turbulence, wobbling, veering, and resistance due to dull edges, improper foiling, or imbalanced camber are readily apparent. A well-shaped blade slices through the water like a knife, quiet and true.

While most paddles have straight blades, S shaping deserves mention. The S offers advantages for novice and advanced paddlers alike. The S cleans up a C stroke wonderfully, exerting corrective "kickout" when trailed. The claw forces a clean entry, even when the paddler is trying to be timid. The S is also a masterful exhibition stick. The claw presents a more vertical blade on extended braces and increases the grab of turning draws at some loss of bracing. S blade shaping dedicates a power face, functioning efficiently only when the cupped face is loaded. The claw's trailing correction to forward strokes increases drag. S shaping compromises inverted jams; the blade's hook curves away from the hull allowing water to flow behind it. S's also veer towards the cupped side when sliced. The S offers advantages and compro-

A double-cambered blade is preferable for freestyle paddling.

mises and is available in straight and fourteen-degree configurations. Try both, you'll want both.

Straight and Bent Paddles

Roughly 60% of a stroke's force is transmitted to the water in the twelve-inch portion of the stroke where the blade is most vertical. The location of this power zone affects the paddler's range of motion and the turning, or torquing, effects of forward strokes. With straight paddles, this power section occurs ahead of the paddler's knee. Bent paddles move the power pulse aft, abeam the paddler's thigh.

Freestyle paddlers usually use straight paddles in solo canoes and a set of matching bents in tandems. The solo's central paddling station offers secure heeling, but the stems are remote and forward strokes tend to turn, or torque, the hull away from the paddle. Straight paddles simplify steerage by locating the power phase of the stroke where it minimizes torque and by reacting the same with either face loaded. In tandems, paddlers are located near the stems and control their boats more easily. They counter each other's torque and often trade the straight paddle's predictability for the bent paddle's advantageous bracing angle and reduced range of motion.

The forward location of the straight paddle's power phase requires more torso rotation to apply power when the blade is vertical. The bent paddle's power pulse is closer to the paddler's body, in better balance, and uses narrower motion ranges of the same muscles. Bio-mechanically, the bent paddle is less strenuous.

Bio-mechanically, the bent paddle is less strenuous.

Like the S, any degree of bend dedicates a powerface—yielding a paddle with one effective blade face and a decidedly inferior back face. The paddle must be oriented properly to load the powerface for most strokes. Most paddles feature offset grips dictating which way to hold the paddle. Visual inspection is easy; the V faces forward. The bent paddle's offset requires the palm to roll. This smoothly inverts the blade to load the powerface on reverse sweeps and prys. Acquiring this simple skill transforms the bent paddle into a magical stick for solo and tandem paddlers.

This is a recent discovery because early bent paddles were racing blades. They veered when sliced, and they didn't have enough blade surface for secure and effective high brace turns. The emergence of larger, double cambered, freestyle blades in bent configuration represents a change in thinking.

Bent paddles enhance the low brace christie by presenting a flatter powerface to the water. The brace becomes firmer and the bite of the paddle can be increased, transferring power into the reverse sweep component of the stroke and improving rotation. The better bracing angle allows greater extension across the rail in tandem moves. Bent paddles facilitate inverted jams because the leading edge more completely intersects the hull for increased deflection. Note: Jamming a bent paddle with the backface loaded means less blade contact or extreme paddler extension.

Bent paddles also alter turning draws. The flatter blade angle to the water improves the move's bracing component but lessens the drawing effect, and bents are difficult to control when slicing in-water recoveries. Bent paddles offer advantages and compromises. They require learning the palm roll to maintain powerface continuity, but everyone should try bent paddles. Bend them at least ten degrees; minor angles do not provide advantages offsetting the complexities of dedicating a powerface.

Bent paddles offer advantages and compromises.

Either solo or tandem bent paddles are useful on tours for their greater efficiency (more speed or reduced effort) and to vary muscle use. Select a large, well-foiled blade, a longish shaft, and a ten-to fourteen-degree bend to retain dominant control at moderate freestyle cadences. Every tourer, solo or tandem, might also carry a small-bladed bent. Its shorter eighteen-inch blade isn't as effective when bracing, but it scratches less across shallows. It also is ideal in those situations where the cadence must be picked up—paddling into a stiff wind, or with miles to go near sundown.

Grips

The paddle's top grip controls blade angle from thirty inches away (Photo 4). Like any other steering wheel, it should fit the control hand comfortably. The grip needs to be a little wider than your hand and deep vertically, allowing thumb control of blade pitch. It should be broadly radiused across the top (say one-half inch minimum), comfortably filling the palm when in a relaxed position. Any additional shaping that improves comfort, control, and the paddler's retention of the stick is welcomed. Most palm grips are symmetrical, so straight paddles may be flipped and either blade face loaded, but offset grips are more comfortable (Photo 5).

By agreeing to hold a paddle just one way and loading only one dedicated face, the grip can be better contoured to fit the hand, improving comfort while reducing fatigue and friction. The resulting grip, with a palm swell and shaped finger relief overhanging the backface, is termed an offset grip. Bent and S paddles dedicate a powerface by blade orientation and should always sport an offset grip. Symmetrical grips are preferred on straight paddles for the versatility of loading either blade face.

Weighting

Blades are larger than grips, and paddles are always blade-heavy. Weighting the grip helps to make a paddle balance better in the hand. Most custom paddles include this detailing, but all grips need attention to improve creature comfort. Strip the varnish off wooden grips before sanding with 320, then 400, grit sandpaper, then oil with Watco or Dekswood. Wipe excess oil off before it sets. On synthetic grips, carefully scrape the molding seams away

All grips need attention to improve creature comfort.

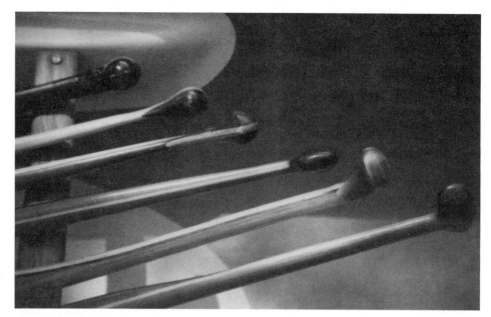

Photo 4: Side view of symmetrical and offset grips

before sanding with 400 grit. Reducing grip friction is well worth the effort. Some paddlers sand and oil shaft grips too.

Shafts

The grip transmits control to the blade through the paddle shaft. The shaft must be comfortable, torsionally firm, and have minimal flex characteristics to perform properly. The shaft should be nicely ovaled in shape to reduce hand fatigue. The dimensions should comfortably fit the paddler's hand. The shaft must be torsionally stiff for precise pitch control and to resist flutter when accelerating forcefully. Test for torque resistance by placing your feet together, slipping the blade tip between them, and twisting the grip. Torsional rigidity is relative so compare several paddles and remember that a paddle cannot be totally torsionally rigid.

A relatively stiff shaft and blade are ideal with slight and even deflection along the entire length.

Test for shaft flex too. Leave the tip on the floor after torsion testing and step back, angling the shaft across your front at roughly forty degrees. Supporting the grip with one hand, place the other halfway down the shaft and press down. A relatively stiff shaft and blade are ideal with slight and even deflection along the entire length. Localized deflection, soft spots, cause flutter and loss of control.

If concerned about stressing your elbow and shoulder, select a smaller blade rather than a soft shaft. Smaller blades slip more when loaded, providing fluid shock absorption. Fit the blade size to your cadence and strength and select a relatively stiff shaft to retain finite blade control.

Because the blade length is already determined, we fit paddles by matching shaft length to paddler torso height and seating stance. Here's how to do it.

Photo 5: Base measurement

Sizing

Sit upright on a solid bench or step and measure from the bench to the bridge of your nose. This is your base measurement (Photo 5). For sport straights, add a couple of inches to arrive at a beginning shaft length. For sport bents, add an inch. Fit touring bents to the base length. Exact fit varies with paddling style and specific canoes. Factors indicating a shorter choice include low seating positions, Canadian-style paddling, preference for in-water recoveries, and paddling loaded canoes. Additional length is suggested by higher seating positions, affinity for cross moves, high kneeling, and paddling unloaded canoes.

Construction

Most canoe paddles are constructed of laminated wood. Strips of various woods are glued together, forming a shaft blank, before grip and blade sections are added. Balanced combinations of lighter and stronger woods are used to the maker's taste.

The chunky blank is then run through various sets of tooling where all the wood not required to make a paddle is removed. Finish methods that resist water and abuse while protecting glue lines are as varied as layups. Construction upgrades include reinforcing tips against riffle chewing by adding cross-laminates, face laminates of veneer, or fiberglass. Top paddles sport hardwood or synthetic edging.

Further improvement in paddle construction will likely take the form of synthetic amalgams. Stronger, lighter, easier to build, and uniformly consistent in physical characteristics, composites are the materials tomorrow's paddles will be built from. Grips can be shaped in molds, the shaft's flex tuned like fly rods, and blades molded to any shape and cross section we desire with fine edges of impact resistant materials. Current synthetic sticks are designed to racing and touring specs, but if there is a demand for synthetic sport paddles, they will be made.

Top paddles will continue with wooden construction, as mold costs limit the ability of synthetics to be precisely fitted to individual size and preference. Superlative custom makers like Wisconsin's Craig Quimby and Florida's Eric Schooley will continue to offer an array of blade and shaft sizing, flex patterns, and grip-fitting options beyond the abilities of production producers. Shaped, sectioned, and balanced to perfection, then finished like fine furniture, the custom paddle is the acme of form following function as art in a tool for demanding paddlers. But experience is a necessary teacher, and we wouldn't know what to order from a paddlesmith without owning and using a closet full of production sticks.

The freestyle blade should match a paddler's strength and cadence.

We need paddles that fit our body size and paddling style in specific hulls, and let's admit we'll need several different paddles. The freestyle blade should match the paddler's strength and cadence. It should be fairly large to provide a bracing surface, sized to not slip excessively at each individual's power level, and shaped to slice smoothly. We need an oval shaft sized to match our hand and stiffened to match individual strength. The grip should be comfortable and controllable, preferably weighted and oiled. It may help if we feel our paddles are beautiful.

So sit to measure, twist and flex to evaluate stiffness, and knife through innocent ponds to evaluate blade shaping. There are lots of great paddles that will enhance your paddling. Take the time to find them.

Clothing, Accessories, and PFDs

Generally, we paddle whenever convenient—an hour after work; a weekend afternoon—and usually in good weather. In much of the country, summer is the most popular season for the sport, and enthusiasts dress for that occasion. They paddle in swimsuits, or shorts and T-shirts, and try to remember to bring a small thwart bag with sunscreen, bug spray, and sunglasses. But freestylists are also a passionate lot and often play with their sport whenever the spirit moves them. Therefore we may need to modify attire for less than ideal times.

Longer outings require additional sun, wind, and bug protection. Long sleeves and pantlegs provide extra protection when crafted of the same blended synthetic materials. Cutting the wind generally provides extra warmth and also yields a sun and bug-proof barrier when needed. Day-long tours may even require an added layer of coated rainwear. This can be carried in a large thwart bag, big enough to hold lunch and camera, too.

In the northern regions, summer is a sometime season. What is the dress code for a "maybe" date in late season, or after season? Off-season paddling offers a spectrum of challenges for the flatwater paddler. The weather ranges from comfortably cool to frigid, and any wind can make the situation uncomfortable, especially when accompanied by falling rain or snow. That's a broad range of potential discomfort, but like the mountaineer and cross-country skier, the paddler needs a handful of layers to maintain a wide latitude of comfort.

Fall is a pleasant season. The sun weakens and the days shorten. While the trees change color, the air grows crisp and the water cools. It sounds inviting, but the cold water could be trouble. It may be fun to practice rolling a hot canoe in a deep pool in August—there are no consequences for

The paddler needs a handful of layers to maintain a wide latitude of comfort.

swimming—but try that in mid-November. Of course, when summer fades, most boaters paddle water that stays out of their canoes and allows them to stay in. So, while you can never completely discount an inadvertent swim, there's no need to suffer the expense and physical discomfort of wet and dry suits.

Inclement weather gear begins with medium or expedition-grade synthetic underwear—warm when covered, fast-drying when accidentally dampened. Modesty and fear of wind chill require a lightweight synthetic shell pullover and pants. Midday sun uncomfortably warm? Strip off the windshell. Colors? Navy blue dries fastest, but is horrible in photo opportunities and may never again be considered stylish. It also will attract the last three bugs left in the county. Please yourself.

Lunch breaks include a welcome respite from exertion, accompanied by a lower energy output and rapid chilling. Solution: the pile jacket. It's the perfect answer to the down versus wool debate of the mid seventies. It's bulky but never heavy, warm even when recently drenched, and it dries rapidly. On colder tours, include a pair of pile or bunting pants. Stowed in a thwart bag, they are lightweight insurance against cooler-than-expected conditions or a partner's maximum credible accident.

The pile layer will keep you toasty through just about anything you'll encounter, unless it's wind and rain or snow. Unsettled fall and early spring weather offer strong arguments for carrying a good rainshell top and bottom. They keep underlying layers dry, warm, and functional. They also provide a wind stop that significantly increases warmth in suddenly frigid conditions. The rainshell can stow with the pile. If unneeded, its just another two to five pounds in that high and dry thwart bag.

Coated garments are less expensive, lighter, less bulky, and more likely to be carried along for surprise use.

Some paddlers have come to prefer non-breathable coatings when likely to spend the day in a rainshell. They seem to leak less than most breathables, and besides, freestylers don't perspire anyway?!?! Coated garments are less expensive, lighter, less bulky, and more likely to be toted along for surprise use. The option of zip-vented jacket sleeves and pants legs is a similar moot point.

Better mountaineering systems offer underarm and leg venting. The zippers add cost and bulk and reduce ultimate thermal insulation, but the trade off in being able to vent excess perspiration and properly regulate your temperature is often worth the other compromises. Paddlers can suffer from the same "I've got to get there today" attitude that drives mountaineers, and a coated rain jacket is in greater need of venting than a breathable one. The same goes for pants.

So, there's a system that works—heavyweight synthetic longies with a lightweight synthetic windshell and pile and rainshell carried as backups (which are pretty much immune to spray and can easily dry to usable condition in case of an accident). But what about extremities? And how do we carry all this equipage?

It is essential that the extremities be protected from the elements. After all, that's where the major heat loss occurs. The head is the easiest part to protect. If you like brimmed hats, take one. They shield your face from the sun, furnish some bug protection, and provide warmth. In extreme conditions take a pile balaclave; it'll also help push a sleeping bag's comfort range downwards.

Hands are a thornier issue, but polypro gloves are useful in cold, wet conditions. Besides, they are also a godsend for friction relief. (Ever take a new paddle on tour without realizing the grip was unsanded and unoiled?) For extremely cold water or weather, better paddling emporiums offer a selection of neoprene gloves and mittens.

Your feet are where you first meet the water. Occasionally a perfect bankside launch can be found, but generally, your feet are going to get wet. Summer paddling is a barefoot sport, or for poptop protection, wear sandals, boat socks, or old running shoes. Off-season, forty-degree water compromises one's elan. Try wetsuit booties, but be prepared, the first shock of wetness is just that—a shock—and the olefactory discomfort builds steadily over time.

The other cold weather foot option is the ubiquitous Bean Boot. We prefer uninsulated versions so dry socks may be applied when one inadvertently steps in over the tops, but remember, boots are tough to swim in.

Those who kneel in canoes for any period of time should consider their knees. Foam-cored hulls may be warm enough, but most composite hulls can get just as cold as the water. Knee pads add lots of comfort to the late season.

A paddler's daypack probably doesn't need to be submersible, but it should secure contents from rain and spray. It doesn't need shoulder straps and can generally be left hanging in the canoe for the few portages likely to be planned into a day's float. Thwart bags are the sport canoe's glove box. They provide easy access to sunglasses, sunscreen, bug spray, car keys, and candy bars. They should attach to thwarts securely enough to resist slippage when the canoe is leaned, and they should affix and release from the thwart easily. Bigger ones will tote foul-weather gear along with lunch, and there are lots of features to choose from.

All paddlers need a functional Personal Flotation Device (PFD) that fits and is comfortable to wear. They'll need it on moving water and also flatwater when weather and wave conditions dictate. Good PFDs are constructed of closed-cell foam encapsulated in a synthetic covering. Choose what you prefer from the broad array of design features, but remember that plastic buckles are easier to work with than knotted ties.

Good PFDs are constructed of closed-cell foam encapsulated in a synthetic covering.

PFD fit is critical. Select a device with enough girth to accommodate pile and rain gear, and enough girth adjustment to fit snugly over a swimsuit. Pay particular attention to adequate armhole sizing, a chafing PFD becomes uncomfortable and unwearable quickly. Pullover designs are lighter and less expensive than zip models, and also offer maximized shoulder movement and improved ventilation. Zippered models offer more convenient entry and egress but weigh and cost more.

Logistics

I n Florida, there's a story that frequently circulates through local paddling clubs—a tale not unlike those told by groups in other parts of the country. Perhaps the story is true and survives as a mild embarrassment to the main characters; or perhaps, like campfire tales from youth, it is merely a product of someone's imagination, designed to spook the observer into hearing "noises."

It seems that a local author of some renown—a freestyle canoeist and a self-styled wilderness paddler well versed in outdoor skills—was preparing for a group outing on Juniper Springs Run in the Ocala National Forest. Pushed by an impatient shuttle car driver, he allowed someone else to tie his canoe to the roof racks, and then, sidetracked by some meaningless diversion, he did *not* double check the security of the attachment. But perhaps his major sin of omission was eliminating the bow lines from the rigging, a decision made in deference to the driver who did not want to mar his car's polished paint job with unsightly rope burns.

A short time later, the car was streaking north on Interstate 95, passing cars and semi-tractor trailers in a fruitless attempt to make up lost time. Unbeknownst to the passengers, the forces of mother nature were hard at work. The constant buffeting from the turbulent air near the trucks pushed and pulled on the extended bow quarters of the canoes. Unsecured with bow lines, the boats slid back and forth. At first the motion was imperceptible, but gradually the oscillations grew in magnitude, and the power cinch knots strapping the canoes to the racks were worked loose.

The next few events seemed to occur instantly—certainly in the barest of seconds. The cinch knots were tied outside of the roof rack towers, so when they loosened, there was nothing to stop them from sliding over the end of the rack. The boat on the passenger's side went first, and as the forward line slipped from the rack, the bow arced skyward. Air filled the inside of the canoe, and the aerodynamic forces increased rapidly. The rear line held taut but the boat twisted up and away from the car. Something had to give!

Finally, the forces exceeded the design limit of the brackets—the rear rack broke loose and vaulted aloft with the canoe. It was about then that the occupants realized their predicament. They watched helplessly as the boat cartwheeled through the air, descending on the paved shoulder at 65 miles per hour. BANG! The stern quarters hit first and the aft air flotation tank burst apart, scattering fiberglass fragments into the wind. Another half flip and the bow augured into the pavement. CRUNCH! Splintered wood railings peeled from the gunwales. The hand-made cane seat swung loose, bounced several times, and slid into the highway. For what seemed like an eternity, the canoe stood balanced on its nose. Then, mercifully, the wake from a passing truck punched it sideways, and it toppled off the shoulder, sliding to a stop in a roadside ditch.

But it wasn't over yet. Although the rear rack had been ripped from the car, the driver's canoe was still attached to the front rack. THUNK! Forces threw it forward and the bow swung hard into the hood, leaving a crater half an inch deep. It recoiled back and the stern quarters were slammed into the roof. CRACK! Then, as the car slowed, the canoe bounced and slid at least six times, leaving deep gouges in the paint.

Now it was over! But not before a great deal of damage had been inflicted on one canoe and the car. And why? Because the driver had been too impatient to allow proper boat handling and because the passenger had not insisted on checking the tie downs.

Luckily the canoe could be repaired and the damage to the car was only cosmetic, though it did require extensive body work. It seems a tad ironic that bow lines would have saved everything but were eliminated so as "not to mar the car's paint job."

Of more import than damaged cars and broken canoes, though, is the possible harm that could come to some innocent bystander.

The safe and efficient transportation of canoes to and from the water is the responsibility of all paddlers.

The safe and efficient transportation of canoes to and from the water is the responsibility of all paddlers. That's what on-land boat handling is all about. Even freestylists must get their craft to the water, and though the nature of their pastime lends itself to local outings on nearby lakes, they must still be concerned with accidents. Problems occur close to home as well.

There are probably as many different ways to transport canoes to the water as there are people thinking about the problem. These range from various roof rack and other car topping systems through the old "shove it in the back of the pickup" method.

The most popular technique involves car topping the canoe with roof racks. These racks can generally be attached directly to the rain gutters. In other systems, they are connected to brackets bolted to the roof of the car or slid neatly into the gap between the door frame and the door.

The first of these alternate mechanisms is called "bronco brackets" and is not a method to be considered lightly since it involves drilling holes through the roof of the vehicle. The second mechanism is called an "aircraft mount" and does not require any adverse modifications to the vehicle (thereby securing its resale value). The bracket design must be tailored for individual automobiles and may require special order.

For the roof rack systems, the canoe is attached to the racks with high-quality line, quarter-inch yacht braid is recommended. It is strong and workable and generally available in most marine/sailing supply stores. Buy it in ten-to-fifteen-foot lengths and have the ends burned to avoid fraying.

Those living in constant fear of their own knotcraft may prefer to select from an array of commercial straps with nearly failsafe buckles. Webbing spreads force loading over a greater expanse of hull than rope, and of course the buckle replaces the knot.

Those living in fear of their own knotcraft may prefer commercial straps with nearly failsafe buckles.

To tie canoes to the topcarrier, use the following tie-down procedure. Attach a line near the center of a rack using a bowline knot. The technique for tying a bowline is described later in this chapter. Do this for both fore and aft racks. (One can leave a small loop made with a bowline knot in one end of the line, looping the line through itself for speedier tiedown.)

Now, place the canoe upside down on the racks with the bow forward and the inside gunwale touching the ropes. Toss each line over the canoe to the outside of the car and secure to the rack using a power cinch or trucker's knot. This knot will also be described later in the chapter. Ideally, this knot will be tied to the inside of the rack towers, although when two boats are tied down, tying outside of the towers may be unavoidable.

Finally, secure the bow to the car frame with two lines. Each line should be attached to the frame or bumper as far to the outside of the car as possible. The bowline is an excellent knot for this application. Pass the other end of each line through the bow carry thwart and pull tight with a power cinch or trucker's knot. *Do not* forget to secure the bow in this manner.

This is an essential step and minimizes sideways motion of the canoe during travel. It also serves as a last-ditch safety device in case of sudden stops. Some car-top systems offer gunwale brackets that clamp to the cross bar, limiting sideways shifting. Shorter canoes may be transported without bow or stern lines on calm days, but high winds still require bow and stern lines lest the bracket dislocate or the carrier's attachment to the vehicle tear loose.

Another common car topping system uses foam gunwale blocks. These blocks fit over the gunwales and the canoe rests on them when it is set on the car roof. When lines are attached between the car and the canoe, the boat is pulled tightly down on the blocks, compressing them.

The two bow lines are tied first using a bowline knot at the car frame and a power cinch knot on the bow carry thwart. Then the two stern lines are attached, also using bowline knots and power cinches. Finally, the tightness on all lines should be adjusted until the boat does not slide on the roof. As an added safety feature, another line could be passed through the passenger compartment and tied around the canoe. Again, commercial straps ease this "belly band" application.

The tie-down lines diverge from each other. This keeps the canoe from moving back and forth. If the tie-down lines are parallel, the only force resisting backward and forward movement is the friction exerted by the foam blocks and this may be insufficient when the vehicle is stopped or slowed suddenly. If it is physically impossible to tie the lines so they diverge, another line (sometimes called a "snotter") can be tied tightly between the rear bumper and the center thwart.

Another ideal arrangement is to tie the bow and stern lines so they diverge as much as possible at the car frame. This large angle stabilizes the canoe and provides greater resistance to sideways motion.

The bowline knot is relatively easy to tie. Many people learned it when they were young and in the scouts or at camp, and use the analogy of the rabbit and the tree. In the old saying, "The rabbit jumps out of the hole, runs around the tree, and goes back in the hole," the path of the confused hare describes the motion of the working end of the rope in the bowline.

To form a bowline, first pass the free end of line around the post you are joining. Next, form a loop in the standing end by crossing the rope. Now pass the free end of line through the loop from below and tuck it beneath the standing end. The free end is now slid back through the loop, this time from the top and pulled tight. The finished bowline knot is especially strong when the standing end is under tension.

The power cinch or trucker's knot is very useful for tightening down loads. To tie it, first pass the free end of line around the post you are tightening to. It is assumed that the standing end is already tied down. Now, with one hand, grab the standing part and twist it twice, forming a loop. Simultaneously, use the other hand to form a bight (an uncrossed loop) between the loop and the post.

Now push the bight through the twisted loop from below and pass the free end of the line through the bight, also from below. Finally, pull the free end until the knot tightens up and the line is taut. The free end must then be secured. A pair of half hitches is ideal for this application.

In the trucker's knot, the bight acts like a pulley in a block and tackle setup. Consequently, a mechanical advantage is created and the user can generate large forces while pulling the knot tight. It also allows tightness adjustment.

The car topping schemes and knots described above, if done correctly, should be sufficient to secure the canoe to the vehicle while it is being taken

The power cinch or trucker's knot is very useful for tightening down loads.

Photo 5: The two-person boat carry.

Photo 6: The overhead carry

to the water site. Once there, moving the boat from the car to the lake is another matter. Although the consequences of screw-ups are not as serious as those depicted above, it may still be a frustrating procedure.

In an elementary sense, this is portaging—only the distances and the loads are no doubt considerably less. Simpler schemes can be used to transport canoe and other equipment to the water.

The two person underhand carry is an excellent technique. Even heavier canoes can be moved over short distances, and because the canoe is turned upright, other gear can be stowed inside. Paddlers carry the boat from opposite sides, left and right, and lift it by the bow and stern carry thwarts.

Multiple canoes can be moved using the two-person, two-boat carry, illustrated in Photo 5. The paddlers stand between the canoes, lifting both by the carry thwarts.

Carrying the canoe stern first allows the portager to stabilize the canoe using the seat.

There are two one-person carry schemes that are quite convenient. The shoulder carry is performed when the canoe is hefted onto the paddler's shoulder and stabilized with the onside hand. Carrying the canoe stern first allows the portager to stabilize the canoe using the seat. This scheme is uncomfortable with heavier boats, although a shoulder pad helps.

For the overhead carry (Photo 6), the elbow of the lower arm is tucked into the paddler's side and the weight of the boat is carried on that arm. The upper arm stabilizes the canoe over the head.

For longer portages, a yoke offers optimal comfort and control. Tandem canoes may have a yoke permanently installed as a center thwart, while solo and combination craft require a dismountable unit. Most yokes clamp to both rails, but some creative units strap around the hull or cantilever from the seat.

Part II: Solo Sport Technique
Or "Who Needs a Paddling Partner, Anyway?"

Beginning Freestyle Solo

Canoeing is our national outdoor sport—an activity indigenous to North America. While often viewed as a means for fishing, camping, or sight-seeing, the canoe can be the prime piece of equipage for a sport as skill-intensive as golf, tennis, or downhill skiing. Actually, we're already there, with college professors evaluating kinesthetics, and coaches and instructors disseminating the most modern information available on how to paddle effectively. It's an exciting time for canoeing.

This chapter provides an informational base for succeeding chapters on strokes and advanced maneuvers. Strokes are the building blocks of canoeing and are learned more quickly in solo boats because there is one person, one paddle, and one hull. The effects, what the canoe does in the water, are obvious.

Stroke descriptions mention large paddle movements. (An example, the sweep is described as a bow to stern arc.) These are conceptual descriptions. Generally, the paddle slips a little from its initial placement position, and the hull moves in relation to the blade.

Strokes are grouped by paddle position. The low brace is described with the sweep, because the paddle is grasped in a similar, low-angled, knuckles-down position. The high brace is described with the draw and the pry (as well as forward and reverse strokes). Cross strokes are logically grouped with their onside variations, but may be ignored initially in the interest of speeding the paddler's progress.

Strokes have three phases: the catch, the execution, and the recovery. The catch describes blade placement and orientation prior to loading. The execution describes force loading the blade and how it moves relative to the canoe. The recovery phase describes preparing for the next stroke.

We have identified four kinds of strokes: bracing, control, power, and

Strokes are the building blocks of canoeing and are learned more quickly in solo boats.

Photo 7

Onside refers to the side of the canoe the solo paddler is paddling on.

corrective. Bracing strokes resist tipping. Control strokes are a pitch or direction applied before the power phase of a stroke to alter the hull's yaw, such as the bow draw component of a C stroke. Power strokes are when the main component moves the hull in a chosen direction, like draws, back strokes, and forward strokes. When power strokes occur behind the hull's center point, corrections must often be made to keep the hull from turning, or yawing, off course, like the outward push ending the C stroke.

Onside refers to the side of the canoe the solo paddler is paddling on, or the bow's paddle side in a tandem canoe, as defined by normal location of the shaft hand and blade. Forward or reverse movement does not change onside/offside. Changing control hands changes onside/offside. Cross strokes, where the blade crosses sides of the canoe and the control hand is not changed, does not change onside/offside terminology.

Dynamic strokes are those where the blade is moved by muscle power, propelling the canoe towards or away from the placement. For static strokes, the blade is held in a stationary position; hull momentum or current provides the motivating force.

The blade has two sides: the powerface and the backface. We usually force load the powerface, but some strokes use the backface, so we mention which face is force loaded. The top hand's thumb, the control thumb, is used in many stroke descriptions as a key to blade orientation or pitch. Normal placement is across the grip, pointing towards the outer blade edge on forward strokes which load the powerface. Occasionally, the paddle is inverted, or turned over, using an atypical blade face. Bent paddles are often inverted to load the powerface rather than the ineffective backface.

Pitches are described at opening or closing angles of attack. Opening placements form an acute, forty-degree angle to the leading stem. They draw the stem to the paddle. Closing angles of attack intersect the keelline at obtuse

Photo 8

angles nearing one hundred and forty degrees, and deflect the stem away from the paddle. Thumb direction helps describe and achieve the proper placement.

The torso features larger muscle groups and is a better source of power than the arms. Lock arms in the position as connective struts, letting the torso pull both paddler and hull to the blade placement. Research indicates the paddle transmits some 60% of the stroke's power in the eight-inch span where the blade is most vertical in the water, so maintaining a vertical shaft and eliminating levering motion increases the efficiency of force transmittal.

When grasping the paddle, the control and shaft hand should be roughly shoulder width apart as in Photo 8. Initially, this seems to be too high for the shaft hand, but it encourages proper use of the arms and allows extended

When grasping the paddle, the control and shaft hand should be roughly shoulder width apart.

Strokes should be practiced and mastered on both sides of the canoe.

reach with the blade. Allowing the shaft hand to creep towards the blade encourages levering with the paddle, which reduces the duration of efficient, vertical-blade presentation.

Strokes should be practiced and mastered on both sides of the canoe. We all aspire to be ambidextrous paddlers, and certainly everyone reduces fatigue by switching sides.

In tandem canoes, the paddlers always paddle on opposite sides of the canoe and in cadence. The bow paddler determines both cadence and side switches because the stern can respond without the necessity for verbal communication.

Strokes for Solo and Tandem Paddlers

The purpose of this chapter is to provide a set of guidelines for an introduction to canoeing. A good foundation of knowledge and solid, high efficiency strokes are important. Let's start by setting some basic rules for paddling.

First of all, we *kneel*, sitting with our knees down and spread to the chines. It's comfortable and stable, and helps control the *heel* of the boat. Sure, we'll sit during sections of day trips or longer tours, but for maximum control, we kneel in our canoe.

Secondly, we paddle from *one side* of the canoe. This means we *never* switch hand positions on the paddle to maneuver. We use cross strokes, we change sides to reduce fatigue, and we practice ambidexterously, but we intend to control the canoe completely without switching hand positions. The key to becoming a skilled paddler is to learn how to control the boat efficiently without changing paddling sides. Couple this skill with the ability to kneel and heel the canoe and your control of the open canoe can become mastery.

Never switch hand positions on the paddle to maneuver.

Let's assume we've delivered a new solo canoe pondside. We gently turn it parallel to the shore and wade out ankle-deep, so the bottom won't scratch when we get in it. How do we do that? We want to stabilize the hull, so it won't roll around as we transfer our weight aboard.

The paddler stands next to the rail, facing the bow. Bending down, he grasps both rails two feet forward of the seat, then using his arms to control roll, he steps into the canoe with his nearest leg, carefully placing the foot just past center. Then, he weights that foot while lifting the second leg aboard. The second foot slides under the seat with weight transferred to that knee before the first foot is slipped back with its knee weighted. The knees are comfortably spread to the chines, the paddler leans against the seat, and he's secure in his canoe.

For a more secure entrance, the paddler may clasp his paddle across the rails under his hands. Orienting the grip at the far gunwale leaves the blade projecting two feet from the shoreward rail. Resting the blade tip on the shore or heeling the canoe until the blade rests on lake bottom allows rock solid security against inadvertent tips.

Tandem paddlers, with a partner to steady the canoe, enter with even greater security. The bow paddler steadies the rails while the stern gets settled, and the stern paddler then braces while his partner comes aboard. This order of entrance is dictated by the stern paddler's wider and more stable stance, greater weight if there is a difference, and ability to see his partner enter the canoe without contortion. But solo or tandem, we kneel when we board our canoes.

With our butts resting comfortably against the seat (or a thwart), it's easy to slide our feet (with our toes stretched out towards the stern) beneath our bodies and spread our knees out into the chines. In this way, we can shift our weight and apply pressure with our legs against the bottom of the canoe and cause it to lean or heel, in either direction.

The fact is, your weight will be pretty well distributed across your behind and knees. When you first learn to kneel, it may become uncomfortable. Your joints will be tight and you'll feel stiff, but it won't be long until you adapt to this new position; kneeling will become second nature.

To comfortably control the canoe through waves, wind, and inadvertent weight shifts, we practice balance drills. While kneeling in your canoe, shift your weight very slowly from one knee to the other. You can shift your weight easily by moving your hips in the desired direction and flexing your waist so your torso remains upright. As you begin to feel comfortable with this rolling motion, gradually increase the amplitude by shifting more of your weight.

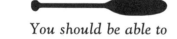

You should be able to lean it in either direction all the way down until the rail touches the water.

In a well-designed sport canoe, you should be able to lean in either direction all the way down until the rail touches the water. Try this exercise. Grab your paddle and hold it parallel to the water with the shaft directed abeam your paddling station. Your shaft hand should grasp the shaft a good distance above the blade. Knuckles should be forward and the hand should be over the water. Your control hand holds the top grip with thumb pointing forwards.

While holding the blade just above the water, slowly shift your weight towards the paddle, onto the onside knee, keeping your torso vertical. Make a vertical line running from the down knee up the leg through your neck. Heel the boat as far as you can. You should be able to get the rail to the water, and once you do, hold it there. This is pictured in Photo 9. The paddle is placed as a brace to keep you from tipping should you bobble.

This position is called a low brace. If you feel yourself going over, you can immediately roll the canoe upright by pushing down smartly with the shaft hand. This pushes the blade into the water, creating a countering force that

Photo 9: The Low Brace.

will roll the canoe in the desired direction. Now, change hand positions on the paddle, trying the low brace on the other side.

When you first feel unstable in the canoe—like you're going to fall out—there is a strong desire to grab a gunwale and pull yourself back in. *Don't do it!* By grabbing a rail, you'll pull the canoe over and still end up in the water. *Use the low brace!*

High-efficiency low braces find both the paddler's hands outside the rail to increase paddle extension. The paddler's head is tilted towards the blade and followed by a hip snap to right the hull. You won't tip over with a solid, practiced, low brace.

You won't tip over with a solid, practiced, low brace.

Sweep

The first stroke new paddlers learn is the sweep. This is quite accidental. What they really want to do is go straight, but the canoe turns away from the paddle. And the object of the sweep stroke is to turn the boat away from the paddle.

The sweep's catch is at the bow with the blade vertical in the water and the control thumb pointing up to load the powerface. As illustrated in Photo 10, the shaft is almost parallel to the water surface. To extend your reach, choke the shaft hand upwards extending the control hand about a foot in front of your waist with the control thumb pointing up. With the shaft arm straight, arc the paddle towards the stern (Photo 11), keeping your nose pointed at the blade. We call this "looking through the stroke," and it encourages torso rotation, powering the blade's arc with the torso muscles. Carry the sweep towards the rear, bending the shaft arm slightly to bring the blade against the stern quarter. (Photo 12). Lift the blade up out of the water,

Photo 10: The Sweep.

Photo 11

Photo 12

while rolling the control thumb forward, and feather the blade flat to the water. Swing the blade forward with torso rotation, letting the tip caress the water surface on the recovery. As the blade nears the bow, roll the control thumb upwards, orienting the paddle for the catch of another sweep. This is the horizontal recovery used with many other strokes, including forward strokes and C strokes.

The sweep is effective throughout its bow to stern arc in a solo craft, but this is not true for tandem canoes. The bow's sweep is effective only for the 90° arc from the bow to her paddling station. The stern's sweep is productive only from his station through the 90° ending at the stern. These truncated motions are called bow and stern quarter sweeps. Tandem paddlers also "look through the stroke," powering the sweep with the powerful torso muscle groups.

Reverse Sweep

As the name implies, this stroke is a sweep done in reverse. This means the paddle is swept from stern to bow and the backface pushes against the water. This stroke is typically used to swing the stern away from the paddle while the boat is traveling backward, making a reverse gradual offside turn. During this turn the canoe travels through a circular arc that opens away from the paddle. The reverse sweep can also be used during forward motion to quickly snap the bow towards the paddle for an onside turn.

To initiate this move, rotate your torso aft until your shoulders are parallel with the gunwale. Extend the paddle back against the stern quarter by bending the shaft arm slightly. The control thumb points, aligning the blade vertically with the backface away from the canoe.

Keeping your face pointed towards the blade and both arms stiff and straight, sweep the paddle forward, moving along a circular arc that extends to the bow. The blade will remain perpendicular to the arc and the torso uncoils to the bow. The reverse sweep propels the canoe backwards, swinging the stern away from the paddle and puling the bow towards it for a reverse, offside turn. With headway, reverse sweeps pull the bow onside while pushing the stern outwards in an abrupt onside turn.

Reverse sweeps pull the bow onside while pushing the stern outwards in an abrupt onside turn.

To recover, lift the paddle out of the water, rotate the control thumb forward so the backface is flat to the water and rotate the paddle towards the stern, where an upwards flip of the control thumb leaves the paddle ready to slip into the water again.

Tandem paddlers limit the paddle's arc to 90°, called reverse quarter sweeps, the bow paddler starts abeam and ends at the bow, the stern paddler starts at the stern and ends abeam his paddling station.

When using a heel towards the paddle to enhance the turning effects of the reverse sweep, solo and tandem paddlers alike often flatten the backface to the water, adding a bracing component to the stroke. This is the reverse sweeping low brace. Apply a secure and quick turn of the paddle to the reverse quarter sweep. Elevate the paddle's leading edge to keep it from diving. As a bow maneuver, this replaces the turning high brace as the eddy move of choice because it has less potential to damage shoulders.

Draw and Cross Draw

The draw stroke is used to move the boat abeam without forward or backward movement, or torque. It's useful for offsetting past an obstruction in the water, leaving or approaching shore, and rendezvousing with other canoes.

The draw stroke is used to move the boat abeam without forward or backward movement

Begin the draw with torso rotation towards the paddle, aligning your shoulders with the rail. With your control hand level with your chin, thumb pointing sternward, fully extend both arms (Photo 13). The paddle is placed vertically in the water, the powerface facing in towards the canoe. Keeping the arms as rigid as possible, pull your hip to the blade with torso rotation (Photo 14).

As the shaft nears the rail, recover for successive draws by turning the control thumb out and rotating the blade perpendicular to the keel. Slice the paddle away from the canoe, while maintaining a vertical shaft until torso rotation and arm length limit further reach (Photo 15). Then roll the control thumb back to catch another draw. This slicing, in-water recovery is particularly quick and will be useful for other strokes, particularly prys and cross forward strokes.

It helps to lift the side of the canoe against which the draw is applied. Elevating the side of opposition allows water to flow under the hull more easily.

Photo 13: A heel toward the onside is more elegant, but less efficient.

Photo 14

Photo 15

A useful variation of the draw is the bow draw. As the name implies, the blade is placed in the water forward of the paddler and drawn diagonally towards the bow, torquing the bow onside towards the paddle. Similarly, a stern draw rotates the canoe offside.

The crossover version of the draw is the cross draw, which moves the canoe abeam to offside. Rotate the shoulders offside and aligned with the keel, swinging the paddle across the hull in a horizontal recovery position. The blade is sliced into the catch, with the shaft arm straight and control arm slightly bent and the shaft vertical in the water. The control thumb points forward, loading the powerface. While uncoiling with torso rotation, performing a hip snap, and drawing the paddle to the rail, the canoe moves smartly abeam to offside. Outward rotation of the control thumb for in-water recovery to successive cross draws is awkward and needs practice to become automatic.

Obviously, tandem paddlers are ideally placed to stroke bow and stern draws. The combination spins the tandem canoe on the spot. For a smooth abeam, one tandem partner must use the cross draw, while the other uses a pry.

Pry

The pry also moves the canoe abeam, but the motion is away from the paddle. It is also useful for offsetting past obstructions, leaving or approaching shore, and rendezvousing with other canoes.

Begin the pry by placing a vertical shaft beside the paddling station and along the gunwale, as indicated in Photo 16. The control thumb pointing back indicates proper blade alignment, with powerface parallel to the keel and backface out. Both arms will be bent, with the paddler's torso facing forward.

Push the paddle away from the canoe (Photo 17) by rotating the torso and straightening both arms. This pushes the boat away from the paddle. Heel towards the paddle, to elevate the side of opposition for increased efficiency. To recover, rotate the blade parallel to the keelline by rolling the control thumb away from the canoe. Slice the paddle (Photo 18), shaft in to the gunwale, re-set the torso, flip the control thumb back, and begin the next pry stroke. Because you are not watching where you are going, glance over your shoulder to see what's coming up.

Bow prys torque the bow away from the paddle, turning the canoe offside, and stern prys turn the canoe towards the paddle. To be effective, tandem prys, also executed perpendicular to the keelline, spin the tandem boat towards the offside. A pry can be combined with a draw to make the tandem abeam.

Photos 16-18 (below):
The pry stroke

Photo 19: The static draw

The Static Draw and Cross Static Draw

The static draw is a flashy way to slip the canoe sideways without moving the paddle. (That's why it's called static.) Of course, nothing comes for free, and in order to create the drawing force, the canoe (and paddle) must be moving through the water. The static draw is an excellent maneuver for sideslipping past obstacles while underway.

With the canoe traveling forward, the boater performs a static draw by first planting a high brace, with the powerface toward the hull and the blade parallel to the keelline (Photo 19). Next, the paddle is rotated to an opening pitch or angle of attack, the control thumb pointing across the stern. The water striking the pitched powerface forces the blade away from the boat. If the blade is placed just behind the boater's hip, the canoe is pulled onside in a sideslip. Move the blade further back and the stern is drawn to the paddle, turning the canoe to the offside. The blade is planted in front of the paddler, and the boat turns onside. Remembering our physics, static draws are more effective when the paddleshaft is nearly vertical in the water and the canoe's side of opposition is elevated.

For an exciting alternative, try the cross static draw. With the canoe underway, simply swing the paddle across the boat (no hand changes), plant the high brace, and rotate the blade until the top thumb points ahead and away from the bow.

The static draw is a flashy way to slip the canoe sideways without moving the paddle.

Static Pry and Cross Static Pry

The static pry sideslips the canoe away from your paddle while underway. Like the static draw, it relies on the canoe's forward motion to create the force to shift the hull.

With the canoe underway, first plant a high brace with powerface toward the hull and the blade parallel to the keelline. Next, point the control thumb back but away from the stern to set the backface at a closing pitch (Photo 20).

Water striking the angled backface pushes the paddle toward the boat. If the blade is placed just forward of the boater's hip, the canoe sideslips offside. Placing the paddle fore or aft torques the canoe. Experiment with different placements.

A cross static pry is a flashy relative of this stroke. Plant a cross high brace, pitching the blade so the control thumb points across the bow.

Photo 20: The static pry

Duffek and Cross Duffek

The duffek is a compound move combining a high brace, static draw, and bow draw for a securely braced, turning maneuver. The duffek is a primary component of many freestyle maneuvers.

The duffek is a primary component of many freestyle maneuvers.

With headway, the duffek is initiated with a static draw. The paddler, maintaining erect posture, rotates his torso to the onside, planting a high brace abeam his onside thigh (Photo 21) and pitches the powerface open, drawing the bow towards the placement. As the rate of turn slows, the paddler opens the angle of attack, arcing the blade forward to gain additional canoe rotation before concluding with a draw to the bow. The duffek may be linked to a deep C for more rotation or to forward strokes to accelerate in a new direction.

The cross duffek is created by linking a cross static draw (Photo 22) with a slice toward the bow followed by a cross bow draw. It requires more balance than the onside move and is less effective because the blade cannot be planted as far from the hull. Initiation with a strong sweep and conclusion to a cross forward stroke go a long way in compensating for the cross duffek's mechanical disadvantages. As a quick pivot for offside maneuvers, the cross duffek is a useful move.

Photo 21 (at left): The duffek

Photo 22: The cross duffek

Forward Stroke and Cross Forward Stroke

The forward stroke is a powerful tool for forward propulsion. The stroke is short, with no correction, and occurs entirely in front of the paddler's hips.

The stroke is short, with no correction, and occurs entirely in front of the paddler's hips.

The paddler first rotates his onside shoulder forward, cocking the torso to drive the stroke and increasing forward extension. Catch the blade perpendicular to the keelline and far enough from the rail so the stroke may run parallel to the keelline without hitting the rail. Both arms are rigid, the shaft arm almost straight and the control arm slightly bent. The short execution is powered by torso rotation.

As the shaft comes past vertical near the knee, the blade is feathered or pitched by forward rotation of the control thumb for horizontal or in-water recovery. Torso rotation carries the blade back to position where an onside flip of the control thumb gives a quick catch to successive strokes. Forward strokes are used in a series with shorter bursts of cross forward strokes to compensate for the bow's tendency to swing offside. Careful attention to keeping the execution phase parallel to the keel, combined with a controlling pitch and offside canoe heel, find the paddler capable of not only running forward without correction, but actually turning the solo canoe towards the onside in a controlled skid. Practice the forward stroke until you can paddle an inside circle, turning towards the paddle.

The forward stroke applies maximum propulsion, but needs modification for cruising with bent paddles. As bent blades are vertical in the water abeam the paddler's thigh, a lessened range of torso rotation is required to reach catch position. That is convenient and paddlers are capable of less torso movement when seated as opposed to kneeling.

The cross forward stroke is an essential tool for the solo paddler. It controls the direction of the canoe while under rapid acceleration. It is a strong initiation for onside moves and a conclusion for many crossing maneuvers.

Start your solo canoe moving with a couple of onside forward strokes. As the bow swings away from the paddle, carry the horizontal recovery across the bow without switching hands. Plant the paddle well forward of the offside knee with powerface aft and the control thumb pointing across the bow. The stroke is short, entirely in front of the paddler's torso. It ends at the onside knee. Then, with a quick forward rotation of the control thumb, the blade is feathered for an in-water recovery to successive strokes (Photo 23).

Cross forward strokes are usually grouped in twos or threes to conclude a crossing freestyle maneuver or to balance the offside swing of a solo canoe accelerating from a dead stop. In heavy water, where the subtleties of the C stroke prove ineffective, the cross forward is used in series for directional control.

Photo 23: An in-water recovery to succesive cross forward strokes.

Back, Farback, and Compound Back Strokes

The back stroke is used to move in reverse, backing away from obstructions or starting reverse movement from a dead stop. It is a quick, short stroke that uses the backface.

The paddler first rotates her shoulders parallel to the onside rail, planting the blade perpendicular to the keelline behind the onside hip. The backface is forward, the control thumb is pointing away from the canoe. The stroke is powered by the torso and runs parallel to the keel. While a horizontal

The back stroke is a quick, short stroke that uses the backface.

recovery may be used, an in-water recovery with the control thumb turned back is faster and preserves some semblance of a brace.

A more dramatic version of the back stroke is the farback. Here, the paddler rotates her shoulders farther onside so the paddle can be planted behind the paddling station. The powerface is forward, the control thumb is pointing across the stern. The farback terminates at the paddler's onside knee, the central hand rotates towards the stern. Feather the blade for an in-water recovery to successive farback strokes.

The compound back combines both farback and back strokes. The standard version requires a blade flip from powerface loading to backface loading at the paddler's onside hip. A new alternative substitutes a palm roll for the blade flip, maintaining powerface continuity.

Both the farback and compound back strokes are elegant, effective strokes. Be careful, though. The dramatic torso rotation and extreme behind reach compromise solo stability. Consequently, they are more often used in tandem canoes.

C Stroke

You've probably seen a solo paddler ghosting along, calmly, smoothly, driving her intimate craft in a straight line. That's the C stroke at work. Also called the traveling stroke and the pitch stroke, it may be the most difficult solo stroke to master and is certainly the most important. Used primarily to travel in a straight line, the C stroke can be changed minutely to turn the canoe in either direction. Variations are also used to link multiple maneuvers together.

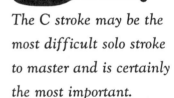

The C stroke may be the most difficult solo stroke to master and is certainly the most important.

First, let's learn how to use it for paddling in a straight line. The diagram in Figure 21 shows that this stroke has three distinct phases: bow draw, power, and stern correction. These phases are connected by smooth transitions and all three phases load the paddle's powerface.

At the start of the first phase, the blade is placed in the water several feet

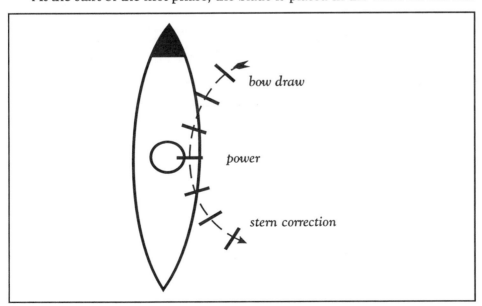

Figure 20: The C stroke

Undesirable swing can be minimized by passing the blade beneath the canoe during the power phase.

in front of the paddler and a short distance out to the side. The blade is pitched diagonally to the keel at a closing angle with the powerface in. By pulling the paddle toward a point in front of the paddler, the boat accelerates forward and turns slightly toward the onside.

During the second portion of the stroke, when the blade is rotated perpendicular to the keelline, the paddle is pulled toward the stern, creating forward propulsion. This thrusting force is well abeam the keel, and the canoe yaws, turning away from the onside. This undesirable swing can be minimized by passing the blade beneath the canoe during the power phase.

If this slight turning overshoots the original direction the canoe was traveling then the third phase of the stroke is required. Phase three is a stern correction—a little outward push that shoves the stern back into line. It's easy to do. The blade is rotated further so the inside edge is behind the outside edge and then pushed ever so slightly away from a point just behind the paddler. If these phases are all done in the correct proportions the canoe will now be "aimed" in the original direction and will be "moving" at speed.

Diagrams are nice teaching tools and useful in explaining why things work. Unfortunately, they don't tell the whole story. For instance, in our example, the diagram illustrates how the C stroke propels us in a straight line. It does not describe how to perform the stroke—what we do with our hands and bodies to produce the desired motion. For that purpose, we will use the photographs shown in Photos 24-26.

At the stroke's catch, the shaft hand is loose, gripping the shaft shoulder width below the control hand with the control thumb pointing abeam. The top arm is extended across the body so the control hand is outside the onside gunwale and approximately nose high.

The paddle is planted several feet in front of the boater and a short distance to the side, as illustrated in Photo 24, and the stroke begins with a diagonal draw. The continuous rotation of the blade as the paddle is moved along the curved path illustrated in Photo 25 is effected by control hand rotation. The shaft hand's loose grip allows the paddle to rotate smoothly inside the palm. Midway through the stroke, the blade is beside the paddler and perpendicular to the keelline.

As the paddle arcs further back the torso is turned onside and the control hand is dropped. This is shown in Photo 26. Paddle rotation continues through the end of the stroke. At that time, the shaft is almost horizontal, with the control thumb pointing straight down towards the water.

Now the stern correction is applied with an outward motion, pushing against the water with the powerface. The stroke is completed by feathering the blade with the control hand, while the shaft hand clears the blade from the water. Horizontal recovery carries the blade forward to a successive catch and turns the torso into position for the next stroke.

There are a few points worth emphasizing. Remember to rotate your torso

Photo 24: Beginning of the C stroke

Photo 25: Power phase of the C stroke

Photo 26: Stern correction with the C stroke

as you apply power. This brings a set of very strong muscles into action and also orients your arm for more efficient use. Second, don't forget to lower the control arm as the stroke progresses. It effectively amplifies the rotation without disrupting the power or contorting your body. Finally, twist the control hand continuously through the stroke, constantly changing blade pitch. It is not possible to rotate the top grip too soon, the prime problem with the C stroke is that paddlers tend to arrive at the control-thumb down corrective phase too late.

By exerting a much stronger bow draw and a harder stern correction,

Twist the control hand continuously through the C stroke.

while also pulling the blade further under the canoe, you can execute a turning C. The result? The boat will make a gradual turn to the onside. Practicing a deep, turning C is a good way to perfect the exaggerated components of the C stroke.

The C stroke is not easy to master, but you must have a solid C to paddle a solo canoe well. Take the time to learn it correctly. Practice it. Work on the arm, torso, and wrist motions carefully. Smoothly and slowly rehearse them in your living room, concentrating on each separate phase.

Tandem stern paddlers need the C stroke too. They delete the initial, drawing phase, but use the execution and corrective portions to counteract the tendency of an uncorrected stern forward stroke to torque the canoe onside.

Reverse C Stroke

There are the practical reasons for running in reverse: to back out of a blocked waterway where it is too tight to spin, or to back ferry away from a strainer. It's also fun and challenging.

The purpose of the reverse C stroke is to propel the canoe backwards in a straight line.

The purpose of the reverse C stroke is to propel the canoe backwards in a straight line. Although the paddle motion is similar to the C stroke, the mechanics are quite different. Primary among these differences is the use of the backface for propulsion. S blades and bents may need to be inverted, loading the powerface.

Initiate this move by rotating your torso toward the paddle and aligning your shoulders with the gunwale. Slip the blade into the water behind your hip and slightly out from the boat. The blade should be almost perpendicular with the water, the powerface away from the canoe. The control thumb points down and away from the canoe, the shaft hand grips the shaft loosely.

The paddle moves through a shallow arc that passes somewhat under the canoe at the paddling station. The first phase is a reverse, diagonal draw, moving the stern slightly to the paddle. Torso rotation powers the stroke, the control hand alters the pitch to keep the blade nearly perpendicular to its arc. As the paddle passes under the paddler, the blade should be perpendicular to the keeline and the control thumb should point directly away from the boat.

Continue to move the paddle forward, rotating the control hand to keep the paddle pitched perpendicular to the paddle's path. When the blade is past the knee and moving slightly away from the bow, the control thumb should point back and down as an outward, corrective pry kicks the bow in line with the stern. To recover for the next stroke, slice the blade from the water, turn it parallel to the surface, and swing it toward the stern.

While reversing, you may wish to turn the canoe onside. Apply a controlling, diagonal draw at the catch and deepen the arc under the hull. Exaggerate the correction to turn the canoe towards the paddle.

Tandem bow paddlers use the reverse J stroke to correct the tendency of other reverse strokes to torque the canoe onside.

Sculling

Sculling is graceful, with smooth fore and aft motions of a pitched blade sideslipping the canoe. The continuous boat movement induced by a scull is an elegant replacement for the sporadic draws and prys.

The sculling draw moves the canoe onside abeam. Begin by rotating your torso onside, aligning shoulders with the gunwale. Slide the blade into the water about two feet behind your hip and a foot away from the boat. Choke up with the shaft hand to maintain a more vertical placement and pitch the blade at a thirty degree opening angle of attack. The control thumb should point across the stern as shown in Photo 27.

Keeping the control hand chin high, slice the paddle forward (Figure 21) and parallel to the keelline. The moving paddle creates a force pulling the canoe towards it. Stop when the blade is two feet forward of your position. Re-pitch the paddle to a closing angle of attack with the control thumb pointing diagonally out and back, and slice backwards (Photo 28). Stop at the catch position and re-pitch the blade for another loaded forward slice.

Pay close attention to the thirty degree blade pitch. Steeper angles move the canoe fore and aft. Tighter pitches dramatically reduce sideways movement.

The principle behind the sculling pry is identical, but it force loads the backface to move the canoe away from the paddle. Initiate this stroke, by placing the paddle in the water, behind the paddling station with the blade pitched at a closing angle of attack. Remember the thirty degree angle! When

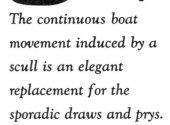

The continuous boat movement induced by a scull is an elegant replacement for the sporadic draws and prys.

Photo 27: The sculling draw

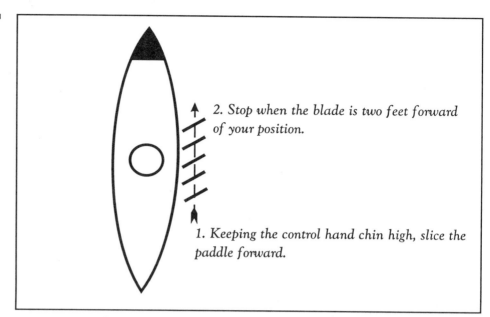

2. Stop when the blade is two feet forward of your position.

1. Keeping the control hand chin high, slice the paddle forward.

Figure 21

Photo 28: The sculling draw

the paddle slices forward, the forces should push the canoe away from the blade. For the second part of the stroke, the paddle is re-pitched to an opening angle of attack.

Learn to scull with the canoe in an upright attitude. Later, you can elevate the side of opposition to increase efficiency. Tandem teams combine sculling draws with sculling prys for abeam movement. Solo and tandem paddlers alike should experiment with cross sculling.

Jam, Inverted Jams, and Cross Jams

Jams are static prys located against the canoe's leading stem (the bow when moving forward). The blade, placed onside at a closing angle of attack, deflects the stem away from the paddle into a quick and violent offside turn.

The jam is sliced forward to intersect the bow quarter from horizontal recovery, the control thumb should point diagonally backwards and away from the canoe. This places the blade against the hull at a closing angle of attack with the backface out.

Inverted jams are planted with the control thumb pointing forward, across the bow of the canoe. The paddle is oriented with the powerface out and pitched to a closing attack angle. While less comfortable to perform, the inverted orientation offers optimal orientation for bent paddles and a concluding sweep with the powerface.

Cross jams are an academically extreme mode of turning the open canoe onside, but they are fun. Operationally, the paddle, when swung across the canoe in horizontal recovery, must be carried almost to the opposite hip before being sliced forward to the jammed placement.

We've described both onside and crossed variations for tandem bow or solo paddlers, leaving you the conceptual task of transposing the movements for reverse solo and reverse tandem stern placements. Reverse and reverse cross jams are fun to play with on a hot summer day.

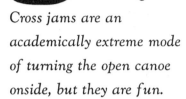

Cross jams are an academically extreme mode of turning the open canoe onside, but they are fun.

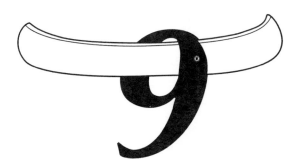

Special Tandem Considerations

Tandem canoes can be fun to paddle. A second paddler provides twice the power, and with a paddler at each end, control over the canoe's direction is enhanced. Interaction between two people can be as pleasant in the tandem canoe as across the coffee table if a couple of simple techniques of interaction are used.

Tandem partners paddle on opposite sides of the canoe, except when a cross move is desired. They paddle in cadence, improving stability and power, and they don't switch control hands to steer the canoe. When touring, the bow will switch sides to ease fatigue and the stern, following the movement, switches too, retaining balance and cadence. The stern follows the bow's lead in establishing cadence and paddle sides.

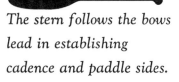

The stern follows the bows lead in establishing cadence and paddle sides.

The stern's position, with the bow paddler in easy view, allows him to read her lead in maneuvering the tandem canoe. No verbal communication is required. The bow, with a better view of obstructions, currents and shoreline, chooses direction using bow corrections. The stern follows the bow's lead, reacting with an array of strokes to complete the bows intended maneuver. The stern has given tactical control of the canoe to the bow in exchange for quiet. No more screaming to the back of the bow's head or straining to hear what the bow shouts into the wind. Tandem freestyle communication is non-intrusive and reactive, with the stern following the bow's lead.

Tandem paddlers use bent paddles. Positioned at the canoe's ends, tandem teams have more finite control over the boat's direction than solo paddlers. Bent paddles exchange an insignificant control loss for a major increase in power and efficiency. Small bends yield a small power increase and more extreme bends increase the advantage. Tandem paddlers use twelve to fifteen degree bent paddles, and the team needs two sets.

Most freestyle moves center upon the combination of a brace and a draw or pry, which requires fairly large blades. Blades over twenty-two inches in length and eight inches in width provide bracing flotation for hanging draws. Recreational paddlers are comfortable with the measured cadence these big blades mandate, but for running in a stiff breeze or slipping across shallows, smaller blades that operate at higher cadences and catch less wind are helpful. So a blade that is eighteen by eight inches proves useful too.

For touring, day tripping and bird watching, we sit on our canoe's seats, but when we're trying a hot move, tandem paddlers seek the security and finite heel control attainable only with their knees in the chines. Knee pads suffice for the stern, but bow paddlers appreciate the increased security of blocks or wedges in the narrowing confines of the bow station.

As in solo paddling, we crawl before walking, and the required interaction within the tandem team suggests heeling exercises and a fair amount of paddling time together before positive and dynamic interaction becomes automatic. That starts with entering the canoe. We place the heavier paddler in the stern, so the bow will more easily rise to waves and react to the paddle.

With the tandem canoe afloat beside the shoreline, the bow paddler steadies the craft as the stern paddler steps in and gets comfortable. Then the stern braces the hull with his paddle while his partner enters. The rational may counter Emily Post, but the stern, with knees broadly spread, is very stable and can see the bow's entry, providing whatever brace may be needed to counter momentary instability. The bow, in contrast, with her knees closer together is less able to balance the hull, and looking forward, will react more slowly to a potential upset.

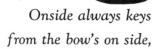

Onside always keys from the bow's on side, even on reverse moves.

Once both paddlers are aboard and stable, the canoe should be trimmed level by adjusting sliding seats or cargo. Then, with both paddlers applying low braces, the team should heel the canoe onside and offside, getting familiar with the canoe's reserve stability before starting to paddle. Note: Onside always keys from the bow paddler's onside, even on reverse moves.

Tandem Forward

The ability to go forward and run a tandem canoe in a straight line is a key skill. Bow and stern strokes need modification to control and power a tandem canoe. Because both paddlers are seated near the stems in the tandem, the rails form an acute angle. They are not parallel to the keelline. Strokes parallel to the rails cause the bow to swing away from the bow's paddle and the stern to pull towards the stern's stroke. The tendencies would counteract, except the stern's stroke ends closer to the trailing stem and generally overpowers the bow.

Both paddlers should align their strokes parallel to the keelline, but correction of the tendency for the stern to overpower the bow may require subtle pitch of the blade too. As the bow rotates her shoulders and torso forward on the horizontal recovery, she plants her blade's catch far enough off the rail to allow a stroke parallel to the keel and almost touching the rail before recovery. Feathering the blade to a closing angle of attack introduces a controlling, drawing component, and pitching the blade to an opening angle yields a prying force. Windage, current, and paddler imbalance may require either pitch to keep the bow on course. As the forward stroke progresses, the bow rolls her control thumb out, flattening the blade for a clean, sliced exit on the horizontal recovery.

The stern uses an equal, mirrored motion, planting the blade perpendicular to the keelline with his shaft vertical at the rail. Generally, the stern rolls his control thumb forward throughout the stroke, introducing a pry component to keep the hull on course. If additional stern compensation is required, the pry is accentuated by an outward push with the shaft hand. This forward stroke with accentuated correction is called a hook stroke. It is used by the stern for forward movement and in its reverse form to correct the bow's tendency to overpower the stern when back paddling.

Tandem paddlers share a dynamic interaction, helping each other guide the canoe and keep it on course. With wind or current overpowering the stern's ability to hook correct headway, the bow automatically tries an opening pitch angle and may even use a partial sweeping stroke to maintain direction. Alternatively, with the stern weathervaning out of control, the bow will introduce a drawing component into each forward stroke, pulling the hull back into line. Similarly, the stern varies pitch and correction from the hook stroke through a partial sweep as required. The stern should develop a hook powerful enough to turn the canoe offside with the bow using an uncorrected forward. Most failures to drive a tandem on a line are attributable to an ineffective stern hook. Start rolling that thumb down immediately after the catch.

Bow Quarter Sweep, Stern Reverse Quarter Sweep

Tandem canoes are turned quickly using the opposing power sources of stern and bow paddlers. The move described in this section turns the boat away from the bow paddler's onside.

A bow quarter sweep combines with a stern reverse sweep as in Figure 22. The bow's quarter sweep starts at the bow and concludes beside her hip, powering the bow away from her paddle. The stern paddler's reverse quarter sweep, starting at the stern and finishing at his hip pushes the stern away from his paddle.

The sum total of these two reactions rotates the canoe to the bow's offside. It is key to perform equal and opposite motions in unison to keep the canoe stable. Horizontal recoveries can be linked to successive strokes if greater rotation is desired. Heeling the canoe to either side increases the rate of spin, as both stems are released from the water, decreasing turning resistance.

It is key to perform equal and opposite motions in unison to keep the canoe stable.

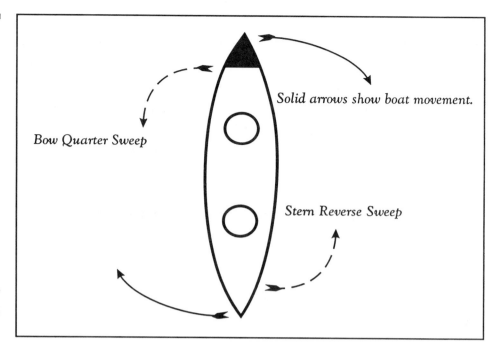

Figure 22: A bow quarter sweep combined with a stern reverse sweep.

Bow Reverse Quarter Sweep, Stern Quarter Sweep

To turn the canoe in the other direction, towards the bow paddler's onside, the bow's reverse quarter sweep combines with a stern quarter sweep, as shown in Figure 23. Notice that the bow paddler's reverse quarter sweep starts beside her hip, finishing at the bow and pulling the bow towards her paddle. The stern paddler's quarter sweep pulls the stern to his paddle.

The sum total of these two reactions rotates the canoe towards the bow paddler's onside. Horizontal recoveries can be linked to successive combinations if more rotation is needed. Rotation and stability are enhanced by matched strokes that are performed in cadence.

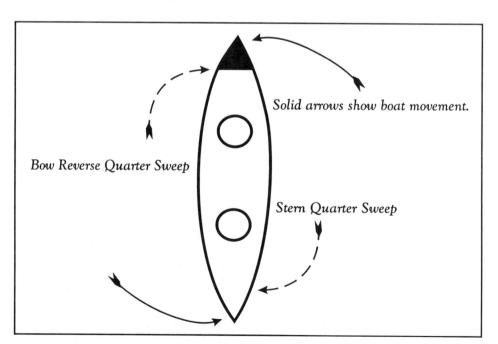

Figure 23: A bow reverse quarter sweep combined with a stern quarter sweep.

Onside and Offside Spins

To spin a tandem canoe onside, both paddlers may employ draw strokes, as described in Chapter 8. The draws should be in cadence, and in-water recoveries are optimal for successive strokes.

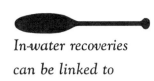

In-water recoveries can be linked to successive strokes.

To spin the canoe offside, both paddlers employ cross draws or prys, as described in Chapter 8. Again, cadence should be coordinated and in-water recoveries can be linked to successive strokes to a smooth spin.

Abeams

Abeam motion, where the canoe is moved sideways without turning, is useful for launching, landing, and offsetting past strainers and other obstructions. Tandem teams balance a draw with a cross draw, or a draw with a pry to move their craft.

Sideslips

A classy abeam movement for a canoe with headway is a sideslip. The bow plants a static draw as described in Chapter 8. The stern matches with a cross static draw or a static pry, carefully adjusting angle and placement to yield diagonal movement without torque.

Sculling

Sculls may be used to replace draws, cross draws, and prys when smooth movement is desired. Described fully in Chapter 8, sculls are an elegant alternative to more forceful strokes.

Back Strokes

Occasionally, every tandem team needs to back up. The paddlers may want another look at an alligator or need to backferry across the top of a rapid.

Photos 29 and 30: Reverse back strokes

When reverse direction is called for, balanced back strokes are the answer.

The back stroke pushes against the water with the paddle's backface while the paddle is moved forward, parallel to the keelline. Both paddlers initiate the stroke by planting the blade just behind their hips. The control thumb points away from the canoe and the blade is perpendicular to the keelline. The stroke is powered by uncoiling the torso with both arms slightly bent, acting as struts connecting the paddle to the torso.

The bow paddler tends to overpower the stern and corrects by rolling her control thumb down and applying an outward hook at the stroke's end. Either in-water or horizontal recoveries may be used for successive back strokes.

When the paddlers need a more powerful reverse, the farback and the compound back are typically used. Both are described in detail in Chapter 8.

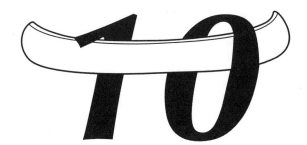

Solo Freestyle Maneuvers

Freestyle maneuvers combine forward or reverse canoe directions and inside or outside heels with paddle strokes that initiate, execute, and conclude the move. We turn the canoe by sticking the leading stem and skidding the trailing stem around it.

Heeling reduces the canoe's in-water length, and as the sides of a canoe are curved, increases the effective rocker presented to the water. Both effects lessen the canoe's resistance to turning. When heeling, we maintain balance by carrying the torso upright and pivoting at the pelvic girdle for a J lean.

In a hull fitted to individual body geometry, we rise off the seat, putting all our weight on one knee and unweighting the other. The torso is erect from the knee to the nape of the neck, and the rail should be stable at the water.

Heels towards the inside of a turn are exceptionally stable. Often we pull the bow inside the turn with a turning draw, but the bow can be deflected into the turn with a jam. In both cases, the stern skids through an arc around the bow. We can also push the stern into a skid with a reverse sweep, forward weighting keeps the bow fixed.

Outside heels are less stable but faster due to an imbalance in frontal resistance. The outer bow plane offers more surface area at a wider angle than the inside one, deflecting or carving the canoe into the turn. Carved turns start more aggressively than inside heeled turns, and the stern skid is faster as the stern is heeled to encourage skidded rotation.

Longitudinal, fore-to-aft weight shifts further enhance freestyle maneuvers. Pitching the hull forward, or bow down, into a carved turn increases both the bow offset, by burying it deeper, and the stern skid, by lifting it higher. Aft weighting has the same effect on reverse moves.

Freestyle maneuvers are good boat handling—whether catching an eddy, eluding a sweeper, or just sliding parallel to shore. They are effective and fun.

Freestyle maneuvers are good boat handling— whether catching an eddy, or just gilding to shore.

We normally practice until we achieve 180° turns. That angle of rotation indicates that initiation, heel, enactment, and conclusion have come together in a pleasing whole. Remember to give the canoe time to complete its maneuver. Horsing the hull is counterproductive. Relax, extend the time duration of the rotational forces, and smooth through the move.

Once a maneuver is completed, the canoe has usually lost its forward momentum. The paddler may resume forward travel, smoothly linking the conclusion to a forward stroke or a C stroke, or may reverse away from the move's conclusion. Reversals include a graceful transition to reverse C, back, or combination back strokes.

We've developed a terminology paradigm to help describe freestyle maneuvers. Freestyle nomenclature seems bewildering. Axle, post, and christie are as intimidating as downhill skiing terms and describe similarly complex maneuvers including an initiation and conclusion, direction of heel and turn, and linkage of several paddle strokes. The following paradigm provides a framework for the language.

We assume that the canoe is traveling forwards, so forward maneuvers needn't be named. Reverse maneuvers are specifically named "reverse." In tandem hulls, the word "stern" indicates reverse direction.

Onside describes a turn toward the side we're paddling on and offside describes a move away from our paddle side.

Because we paddle ambidextrously, we use onside to describe a turn towards the side we're paddling on and offside for a move away from our paddle side. Tandems key onside off the bow's paddle side for forward and reverse maneuvers. Cross strokes, planting the paddle across the hull without changing control or shaft hands, do not effect onside and offside labeling.

We usually heel the canoe, reducing turning resistance, freeing the stems, reducing in-water length, and rockering the hull's bottom shape. We can heel the hull into the turn for a stable skid, or outside, away from the turn, starting the stems carving.

Having addressed the hull's direction of movement, turn, and heel, we need to agree on conventions describing paddle strokes. The paddle will usually be onside, but we mention cross strokes such as a cross draw. And assuming dynamic movement of the paddle is the norm, we mention static plants like a static hanging draw.

Freestyle maneuvers combine several distinct strokes, listed in order, with descriptions of how they are linked. For example, a turning C Stroke, palm roll linked to a low bracing reverse sweep would be graphically shown in the paradigm depicted in Photo 31.

To reduce redundancy, we've developed one or two word names for more common combinations or maneuvers. Variations from basic turns are noted. Tandem turns are always described for the actuating paddler, and trailing moves listed secondarily, except that the direction of turn remains keyed to the bow's paddle side.

Axle—An onside maneuver, heeled into a duffek.

Cross Axle–An offside move, heeled into a cross turning draw.

Post–An onside maneuver, heeled away from a turning draw.

Cross Post–An offside maneuver, heeled away from a duffek.

Christie–An onside move, heeled towards, into, a turning C, palm roll linked to a low bracing reverse sweep.

Reverse Combination–A christie linked to an axle.

Outer Gimbal–A reverse combination to a deep C, to a christie for a 360° turn.

Inner Gimbal–A christie linked to low angle 360° circle sweep under hull.

Wedge–An offside maneuver, heeled away from the turn, enhanced by a jam, inverted jam paddle placement.

Cross Wedge–An onside move, heeled away, and towards the cross jam.

Reverse–Added to basic maneuvers to describe motion towards the stern.

Bow–Indicates forward tandem maneuvers, but is often silent.

Stern–Flags reversing tandem moves, but we still key onside and offside to the bow paddler. Tandem, stern maneuvers are seemingly mirror imaged. (For example: a stern axle is an offside move.)

Axle

The axle is the signature freestyle maneuver. Characterized by a dramatic inside lean and secure turning high brace, the axle is an elegant onside turn.

From forward travel, initiate the axle with a turning C, accentuating the depth and stern correction of a forward stroke. This starts a gentle onside turn. During horizontal recovery, heel the canoe onside, freeing the stems and reducing turning resistance. Heel the rail down to the water, flipping the control thumb from forward to point at the onside shoulder while planting a turning high brace abeam and just into frontal resistance (Photo 31).

The Axle is a signature freestyle maneuver . . . an elegant onside turn.

Photo 31: The Axle

Photo 32: The Axle

Keep the shaft hand loose so the shaft rotates easily and keep your torso vertical by pivoting at the waist. The static portion of the turning high brace draws the bow into the turn and encourages the stern to skid away. This can be enhanced by a forward weight shift. As the turn slows, open the blade's powerface prolonging rotational motion (Figure 32).

Conclude the axle with an arcing draw to the bow, linking to a C stroke. The paddler may wish to reverse away from the axle. For a reversal, the paddler slices the blade towards the stern, with the control thumb pointed back, flipping it outwards for successive back strokes.

Post

The post is a quick and secure move used for eddy turns and plain fun.

The post offers freestyle paddlers an aggressive onside move that takes advantage of a canoe's tendency to carve into a turn when heeled away or outside it. It is a quick and secure move used for eddy turns and plain fun.

Initiate the post by accentuating a C stroke into a turning C and emphasizing the outward stern correction at stroke's end. Heel the canoe offside, the rail flush to the water, by pushing the offside knee down while lifting the onside leg.

The stern correction and the extreme heel start the bow carving onside. While maintaining the offside heel, recover the paddle planting a duffek over the high onside rail. The water strikes the powerface, pulling·the bow farther into the turn as the stern skids free. When the turn slows, conclude the post with a bow draw, heel the canoe upright, and recover into a forward stroke or link to back strokes for a reversal.

The post is a quick eddy move because the downriver lean keeps the hull dry while the carved deflection helps an underpowered solo canoe cross eddy lines with authority. The post is greatly improved by weighting forward to

Photo 33: The Post

pitch the bow down. This increases the bow's deflection into the turn while lifting the stern higher.

Wedge

The wedge is a fast, flashy offside move using an inverted jam to deflect the bow into a dramatic, skidded carve away from the paddle. With the outside rail heeled flush to the water, a wedge snaps the canoe through such a sudden skid that the unwary may find himself counting fish.

A wedge snaps the canoe through such a sudden skid that the unwary may find himself counting fish.

While traveling forward at speed, initiate the move with a broad sweep. This starts the canoe turning offside. An onside heel offsets the bow into the turn, starting it carving while the paddler begins a low horizontal recovery. Keep the heel smooth—bobbling causes turbulence and slows the canoe.

Use off-horizontal recovery, weight forward and drop the shaft hand while knifing the blade into the water at a closing pitch, powerface out. The leading edge slices to jam against the hull, deflecting the bow further into the move. Watch for a twitch when the inverted jam meets the rail. The bow is offset into the move so firmly that paddlers often inadvertently exit the canoe, but the prepared may ride the tightening skid past 180°, concluding with a sweep as the hull is heeled upright.

Many paddlers employ a jam, with the powerface against the hull, the backface loaded, and the paddler palm rolling to the concluding sweep. With bents, the sweep is less effective due to the disadvantageous angle of the backface.

Wedges are ideal reversal maneuvers because, though abrupt, they leave the hull without further momentum. To link to reverse travel after the concluding sweep, palm roll to an inverted reverse C, loading the powerface, or slice to catch position for back strokes.

Riding through the cross axle, the canoe gracefully rotates, first showing its curved underside and then slowly revealing its interior.

Cross Axle

For a cross axle, the canoe is heeled to the offside rail, the paddler twists into a cross move, holding the shaft high and fixed. Riding through the maneuver, the canoe gracefully rotates, first showing its curved underside and then slowly revealing its interior. The cross axle is an elegantly pleasing move to watch and perform.

The paddle is crossed to the offside without switching hand positions on the shaft. The canoe is heeled offside into the move, creating an axle as the boat is heeled toward a turning high brace.

Initiate the cross axle with a sweep, like other offside moves. As the bow begins to turn away from the paddle, the canoeist slices the blade out of the water, feathering it, control thumb forward. While rotating the torso offside

Photo 34: The Cross Axle

Photo 35: Completing the cross Axle

and heeling the offside rail down, the paddler swings the blade across the bow, planting a turning high brace abeam the offside thigh. The shaft hand can choke up on the shaft to increase extension.

Offside, crossed heels are executed by hinging the body at the waist and keeping the upper torso vertical. Holding the lean during a cross axle is ticklish but there are some tricks that might help. While learning the move, try staring at the offside rail as it hugs the water. Any motion is immediately observed and corrected with knee pressure. Once comfortable with the cross heel, try weighting forward by raising off the seat and transferring body weight to the knees. This lifts the stern higher, reducing its resistance to rotation.

Ride the cross axle until rotation slows or the canoe has completed the desired turn. Then conclude by cross drawing the blade to the offside bow, swinging the paddle over the boat. Finish with a forward sweep before continuing into the next stroke. This technique extracts a little more rotation out of the maneuver.

As an alternate recovery, try linking the cross draw with a cross forward to accelerate the canoe forward or even initiate a successive onside move. This technique stops the rotation but allows a more precise, powerful finish.

Cross Post

The cross post is a stylish maneuver that turns the canoe quickly and precisely offside. It is based on a cross duffek and the inherent characteristic of a canoe to spin faster when heeled outside a turn.

While underway, initiate the cross post with a sweep, while heeling the canoe onside until that rail touches the water. This deflects the bow inside the turn, starting the canoe carving offside. Bring the paddle forward in a horizontal recovery, swinging the blade across the hull with similar torso

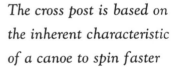

The cross post is based on the inherent characteristic of a canoe to spin faster when heeled outside a turn.

Photo 36: The cross post

rotation. Loosen the shaft hand, planting a cross turning high brace, or duffek, abeam the paddling station. The control thumb will point forward, away from the bow. The pitched, static draw pulls the bow farther aside while the stern skids out.

Weighting forward is particularly helpful in increasing bow offset on outside heeled maneuvers, so come off the seat and ride the cross axle. As the move slows, slip the blade forward, opening the angle of attack. Then, roll the hull upright and conclude with a cross draw to the bow. Follow the draw with a cross forward stroke before crossing the paddle back onside and resuming the C stroke. An interesting reversal is slicing from the cross bow draw to cross farbacks to initiate a reverse onside maneuver.

Cross Wedge

Wedges are not impossible moves—just difficult, especially cross wedges! Given that the paddler is crossed to the offside on a wildly skidding maneuver based on the cross jam, it's easy to imagine this stroke being a little more difficult.

Wedges are not impossible moves—just difficult, especially cross wedges!

The cross wedge turns the canoe onside, exactly the same as the axle and the post, and it is similarly initiated with a hard correction at the end of a turning C. This starts the bow carving to the onside, which is accentuated as the paddler heels the offside rail to the water.

The paddler then slices the blade from the water, feathers it on horizontal recovery, and swings it across the bow. As the blade crosses over the offside rail, the paddler lifts the control hand until the shaft is vertical and perpendicular to the water. The control thumb points forward and the torso has been rotated towards the offside rail.

The paddle is then planted next to the gunwale and forward of the

Photo 37: The cross wedge

paddler's knee at a closing angle of attack (Photo 37) in a cross jam. Water pressure loads the backface, pushing the blade and the canoe farther into the turning move. This force comes on quickly, literally snapping the bow into a radical deflection inside the turn.

Practice your first couple of cross wedges with minimal headway to ease the offset. After getting comfortable with the move, weight forward off the seat to increase the bow's rate of carve.

Ride the cross wedge as long as the canoe has any momentum, but when rotation stops or the canoe has turned the desired amount, conclude with a cross bow sweep. If using the cross jam, rotate the control thumb in to point down, palm rolling halfway through the cross sweep before successive cross strokes. Then swing the blade back onside, continuing with forward motion.

Paddlers, particularly those using bent paddles, may prefer to turn the powerface out for the inverted cross jam. Palm roll once the paddle is crossed, and again for the concluding cross sweep.

Palm Roll

The palm roll is a key freestyle technique linking strokes and maneuvers by smoothly maintaining continuity of powerface. This allows rotational and bracing forces to be sustained throughout stroke changes. As an added feature, it also allows the canoe to be leaned farther and turned through greater angles of rotation.

Hand control is essential and the proper grip is critical. The shaft hand must grip the shaft loosely enough to allow the paddle to pivot and the control hand must be free to ease around the grip. The basic exercise for learning the palm roll is to link a C stroke with an inverted, low bracing reverse sweep to a duffek to another C stroke.

Hand control is essential and the proper grip is critical to the palm roll.

At the conclusion of the C stroke, the control thumb points down and the blade's powerface is away from the canoe. Loosen the control hand, and without turning the paddle, rotate the hand so the thumb points up. Move to a knuckles-down control hand grip and push the flattened blade through the inverted, powerface-loaded reverse sweep with a loose shaft hand. As the blade comes abeam, increase the shaft angle by elevating the control hand. Rotate the shaft hand to the outside of the shaft and apply both forward and inward pressure while linking to a turning high brace.

Loosen your fingers, rotating the control hand (Photo 38) 180° until in a thumb-aft, high brace configuration. Now, conclude the move by drawing the paddle toward the bow and linking with another forward stroke. The maneuver just described is the reverse combination.

The inner variation of the palm roll is more difficult to learn but just as useful. Linking a deep C stroke to a reverse sweeping low brace, a duffek, and a bow draw is the sequence of the outer gimbal, good practice for palm rolling.

To learn the reverse palm roll, start at the conclusion of a reverse C. With

Photo 38: Forward palm roll

Photo 39: Forward palm roll

S and bent paddles inverted, roll the control thumb down, orienting the blade vertically while maintaining force on the powerface (Photo 39). Note: You'll invert these sticks for the reverse C, but use the backface of symmetrical, straight paddles.

Do not flip the blade over to relieve wrist stress. Loosen the control hand, rotating it across the grip into a comfortable thumbs-up attitude as the blade is powered into a sweep by the shaft hand (Photo 40). The powerface will flatten on the water, providing a low-angled brace, the control hand is in a high brace orientation.

Practice the reverse palm roll slowly and carefully, remembering not to flip the blade over. Increase power and heel towards the paddle as muscles become programmed.

Photo 40: Reverse palm roll

The palm roll is an essential repertory move for advancing Freestylers. It maintains powerface continuity through stroke transitions, keeping bracing and rotational forces active so the canoe can be heeled and turned farther. Forward or reverse palm rolls require loose hands on the paddle so the shaft can pivot as the control hand eases around the top grip. But palm rolls can be practiced on dry land without fear of counting fish.

A great way to learn forward and reverse palm rolls is on the beach with a ball or apple. Standing, drop the object near your feet. Grasping your paddle normal position, move the item clockwise in a one-foot diameter circle, touching it only with the powerface. A loose shaft hand allows the control hand to finger rotate the grip, maintaining powerface contact with the object. Once comfortable, roll the item in a counterclockwise circle. That's the reverse palm roll if you're paddling on the right! Then switch hand positions on the paddle to learn forward and reverse palm rolls on the other side of the canoe.

Low Brace Christie

The low brace christie is an advanced version of the reverse sweeping low brace. The christie keeps the powerface loaded, palm rolling from a deep C to an inverted reverse sweeping low brace. This smoothly maintains bracing and turning forces for a more secure, higher-angle maneuver. Loading the powerface of bent and S paddles for enhanced efficiency, the palm roll is a favorite onside move of advancing paddlers.

The low brace christie is a favorite onside move of advancing paddlers.

From forward travel, initiate the christie with a deep C stroke while leaning the onside rail to the water. As the blade comes vertical during the stern correction at the C's conclusion, the control thumb will point down. Continue outward pressure with a loose shaft hand. With a subtle, rolling

Photo 41: The low brace christie

Photo 42

Photo 43

pressure, the shaft hand starts the blade easing over to the flat angle needed for a reverse sweeping low brace. The powerface addresses the water. Palm roll the control hand to a thumb forward position. The canoe will turn on its own, but as the rotation slows, the motion is enhanced by a reverse sweep. Elevate the leading blade edge to resist diving and maintain a low brace.

The christie fades as the reverse sweeping paddle comes abeam, generally after turning the canoe through 90°. Because the canoe loses most, if not all, headway, the christie offers an ideal maneuver from which to initiate reversing maneuvers. Slice the paddle back to the catch position for a reverse C or back stroke.

The christie serves tandem paddlers as an ideal stern correction for onside maneuvers and is especially effective for asymmetrical touring solos whose longer bows are resistant to the entire series of bow drawing turns based on the duffek. The christie lets the bow set itself as the stern is kicked into a skid by the reverse sweep.

Christie/Axle Reverse Combination

Often, when an acute turn is required, no single maneuver is sufficient, but we can link complementary maneuvers. Blending the christie with an axle allows rotation past a 180° turn that neither maneuver can yield alone.

Blending the christie with an axle allows rotation past a 180° turn that neither maneuver can yield alone.

While traveling forward, initiate the christie with a turning C while heeling the onside rail. Palm roll from the C stroke into an inverted reverse-sweeping low brace. This kicks the stern into a skid while the low brace secures the heel, which frees the stems and reduces turning resistance.

As the paddle sweeps abeam, the christie loses rotational impact. Palm roll from the control thumb forward, low brace position to a thumb aft, high brace posture, as shown in Photo 44. Continue the lean and apply a static turning high brace. This pulls the bow into the turn, extending the stern's motion. As the momentum drops, open the powerface to an even greater angle and move the blade forward. Finally, conclude the maneuver with a bow draw and link it to a forward stroke, or initiate reverse travel with slice to a back stroke.

The reverse combination links several maneuvers and allows the paddler to turn past 180°. Offering a smooth and efficient way to extend a christie, it comprises the initiating half of the gimbal and is an effective eddy turn.

Photo 44: The christie/axle reverse combination

This is a graceful move, the canoe cutting a perfect circle around the paddle.

Reverse Axle

The reverse axle mirror images the axle. Executed while the canoe is moving in reverse, it is an onside turn, rotating the leading stem (the stern) towards a duffek. The canoe is heeled onside, defining the axle. This is a graceful move, the canoe cutting a perfect circle around the paddle.

The reverse axle initiates from the reverse C or back stroke. The last stroke before the axle would be a reverse turning C, starting the canoe into the maneuver. The backface pushes the bow into a skid and the control thumb points down and to the rear. The canoe is heeled onside towards the paddle, until the rail touches the water.

The blade is sliced aft and planted directly abeam the paddler's station, the powerface is pitched open with the control thumb pointing aft and away so the stern is drawn towards the paddle and into the move (Photo 45). The canoeist rides the turn out, as shown in Photo 46. When the turn slows, it's time to conclude the maneuver.

With extreme torso rotation, the paddler executes an arcing draw to the stern. When the draw approaches the stern, palm roll the control thumb abeam for successive back strokes, or for reverse C strokes.

When comfortable with the reverse axle, try linking it to other moves and creating complex maneuvers. For example, if your recovery includes a reverse

Photo 45: The Reverse Axle

Photo 46

C followed by a forward sweep and forward strokes, you've executed a reversal, gracefully transitioning from a reverse skid to forward travel.

Reverse Post

During an axle the canoe heels towards the turning high brace while during a post it is leaned away from the paddle plant. This holds for reversing maneuvers too, so except for the direction of heel, the reverse post should be almost identical to the reverse axle. The purpose of the two maneuvers is the same—to turn the stern to the onside—but the outside heel's deflection makes the reverse post a quicker move.

Initiate the move with a hard outward correction ending with a reverse C stroke, then weight your offside knee, heeling the canoe outside its turning arc. Torso rotate onside, swinging the paddle aft and planting it over the high onside rail, abeam the hips in a reverse turning high brace. The blade angle is correct when the control thumb points aft and away from the canoe. Proper form for this phase of the reverse post is shown in Photo 47. Note the paddle shaft is more vertical than in a reverse axle.

The paddle shaft is more vertical in the reverse post than in a reverse axle.

The reverse duffek pulls the stern toward the paddle while the bow skids around, the paddler simply riding the turn and enjoying the graceful motion. In conclusion, increase torso rotation to power an arcing draw to the stern. As the draw approaches the stern, heel the canoe level, rotate the paddle perpendicular with the keelline, the control thumb pointing abeam, and continue into a back stroke or reverse C.

Practice slowly and deliberately to master this move. Then begin linking the reverse post with other maneuvers, creating an array of combinations. Reversals, linkages to forward moves, are achieved by slicing forward from the concluding draw to the catch point for forward strokes.

Photo 47: The reverse post

The reverse wedge is a snappy, tight turn, easily rotating the canoe past 180°.

Reverse Wedge

Everyone remembers counting fish when learning wedges, and that was forward wedges. Surely the reverse wedges must be an order of magnitude harder to learn? Well, not really. The reverse wedge is an exciting and elegant move to learn.

The reverse wedge is a reversing move, deflecting the stern offside, away from a stern jam while the bow skids around it. It is a snappy, tight turn, easily rotating the canoe past 180°.

To initiate with a reverse sweep, the boat is heeled to the onside by weighting the onside knee and the stern begins carving offside. The canoeist recovers from the reverse sweep by slicing the blade towards the stern. The powerface is against the canoe, the control thumb points up and aft.

The slice stops at the rail, aft of the paddler, in a jam. The blade is pitched to a closing angle of attack by rotating the control thumb to point across the stern. Water pressure loads the backface, deflecting the stern further inside the maneuver. Both hands should be held across the gunwale and over the water, while the shoulders are turned towards the paddle. Note: Paddlers using a bent shaft will prefer an inverted jam, with the powerface set out.

Palm roll into the paddle placement. Ride wild and unbraced, as far as the turn goes, before concluding by smoothly transitioning into a reverse sweep. Then slice aft to continue with reverse strokes. A reversal to forward movement is particularly easy, flipping the paddle to catch a forward stroke rather than recovering for successive reverse strokes.

It is important to maintain a constant onside heel as bobbling causes turbulence that slows rotation. Also remember to start setting the jam, or inverted jam, with slight angles of attack. Extreme angles increase the jump when the shaft hits the rail and slow or stop the canoe.

Reverse Cross Axle

The reverse cross axle is an offside reverse maneuver skidded around the paddler's reversed and crossed turning high brace. It is initiated from reverse steerage by heeling the canoe offside while completing a reverse sweep, which starts the hull turning offside. As the paddler carries his blade across the canoe with torso rotation, he slices into a cross duffek pitched to an open angle of attack towards the stern.

Ride the position as long as possible while momentum fades before arcing the paddle into a cross draw to the stern with increased torso rotation. From the concluding stern cross draw, link to a cross farback before recovery onside to continue reverse travel, or slice the paddle forward for a series of cross forward strokes before recovery onside to forward travel.

Reverse Cross Post

The reverse cross post mirrors the reverse cross axle as a reversing, offside move except that the stern is carving into the maneuver due to the outside heel. Paddle placement is somewhat more vertical, because the paddler is reaching across the high side of the canoe and because the concluding cross draw to the stern is more of a loaded slice than an arcing draw.

Reverse Cross Wedge

The reverse cross wedge is an extreme cross maneuver. The paddler rotates his torso offside to place an unbraced jam on a radically heeled rail. It is thrilling and offers graceful linkage to successive moves.

This is a reverse move, swinging the stern towards the paddler's onside—the same intention as the reverse axle and reverse post. As with other reverse onside turns, the reverse cross wedge initiates with a hard bow correction to a reverse C stroke. The paddle is then sliced out of the water and swung across the bow, while the canoe is heeled offside and away from the maneuver.

While torso rotating offside, the canoeist slices the paddle to intersect the gunwale behind his hips in a stern cross jam. The blade is pitched to a closing angle with the control thumb pointing forward and abeam, loading the backface and increasing the stern's deflection inside the move. (Paddlers, particularly those using bent paddles, may prefer an inverted cross jam, loading the powerface by palm rolling the control thumb forward and away.)

Gently increase the blade's pitch while enjoying the thrill of a wild, reverse skid (Photo 49). Conclude the reverse cross wedge by continuing the turn with a cross reverse sweep. Recover to reverse travel by slicing towards the stern for cross back strokes, or switch to forward travel by rolling the control thumb out for cross forward strokes. Cross the blade back over to onside after initiating motion.

Photo 49: The reverse cross wedge

Reverse Christie

How about a flashy reverse maneuver based on the reverse palm roll? We call it the reverse christie. Moving in reverse, initiate the move with a deep reverse C stroke, arcing the blade deep under the hull while leaning the boat onside. Then kick the bow into a skid with a powerful, thumb-down correction. Maintain the force on the powerface, palm rolling into a broad sweep from bow to abeam the paddling station. This keeps the bow moving around the stern in a fast skid.

Linking the reverse christie to a reverse axle extends rotation. As the blade comes abeam, bring the control hand up from the low brace position into a reverse turning high brace. conclude the move with an arcing draw to the stern.

The achieved angle of turn is determined by how slowly the sweep is executed and how well the inside heel is maintained without bobbling. Put another way, don't force it. Let the boat make the turn with a little help from your knees and paddle. To increase drama, hold the high brace as a static position before concluding the sweep.

As the sweep ends, the canoe is virtually dead in the water. The canoeist can follow the sweep with C strokes for a reversal to forward motion, or the paddler can initiate back strokes to gain headway linking to a successive reversing move.

You can also continue the maneuver, keeping the hull leaned, and palm roll right into another reverse deep C. If you continue this sequence, you can effectively auger the canoe backwards into the swamp in a maneuver called the reverse gimbal. It's a great way to practice the palm roll.

Inner Gimbal

In technical circles a "gimbal" is a precision mechanical instrument used to smoothly and accurately rotate a platform. It consists of an axle, a frictionless bearing, and a motor to drive the angular motion. It is not a coincidence that a group of freestyle moves were also designated "gimbals" because they were named by a pair of engineers who saw the uncanny resemblance with their mechanical brethren.

The gimbal is one of those freestyle moves that is done for the sheer fun of it. The idea is to rotate the canoe through tight, precise orbits. The paddle is the drive motor and, as it moves through a complete circle, it pushes against the water, creating a turning force. For an "inner gimbal" the paddle is almost completely immersed in the water so the shaft is horizontal and the blade traverses a large circle, as illustrated in Figure 24.

The inner gimbal turns the bow to the onside. It is based on the palm roll and the powerface is always loaded. Initiate the move by heeling the canoe to the onside rail. With both hands over the side of the boat, immerse the paddle

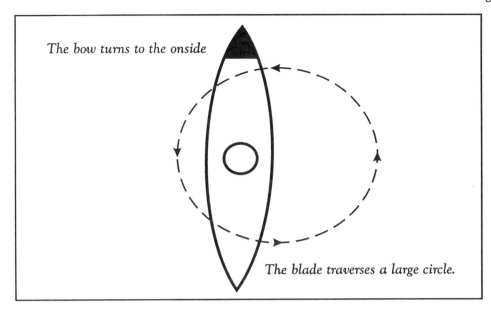

The bow turns to the onside

The blade traverses a large circle.

Figure 24: The inner gimble

fully in the water with the blade aft of your position. The powerface is away from the canoe and the control thumb points up.

Sweep the paddle toward the bow (Photos 50 and 51). As the paddle nears the bow, palm roll your control hand until the thumb points down, as in Photo 52.

Draw the blade to the bow and complete a deep arc under the canoe. Ideally, the blade passes beyond the offside gunwale. As the paddle passes back to the onside and is pushing away from the stern, your control thumb points down. Another palm roll orients the thumb upwards and the paddle is ready to enter another cycle.

When your paddle is under the canoe, especially when the boat is leaned all the way to the water, you have nothing to brace with. Good balance skills

Photo 50: The inner gimble

Photo 51: The Inner Gimble

Photos 52

compensate for small (or maybe large) canoe movements. Don't be surprised if you swim while learning this move.

A reverse inner gimbal is used to rotate the stern towards the onside. It is based on the reverse palm roll, and as the blade traverse the large underwater circle, the backface is loaded, although the paddle, especially bents, may be inverted to use the powerface.

Outer Gimbal

In some mechanical devices an inner gimbal is nested inside an outer gimbal and the whole device can be rotated independently about two different axes. In marine applications, such mechanisms are used to isolate navigation

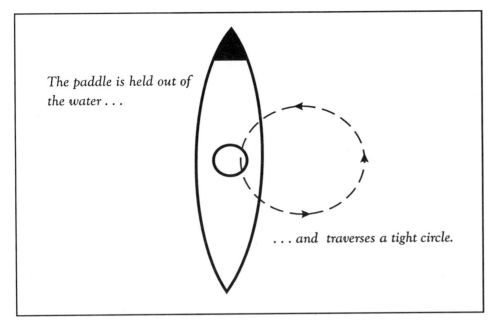

The paddle is held out of the water . . .

. . . and traverses a tight circle.

Figure 25: The outer gimble

compasses from the pitching and rolling motions caused by rough seas.

For freestyle paddlers, the purpose of an inner and outer gimbal is the same—to spin the boat onside for no apparent reason other than to have fun. The difference lies in paddle placement. An inner gimbal is executed with the paddle fully immersed *in* the water in a low brace position, an outer gimbal is executed with the paddle held well *out* of the water. In contrast, the shaft is nearly vertical and in a high brace position, and the blade traverses a much smaller circle as illustrated in Figure 25.

The outer gimbal turns the bow to the onside and is based on the palm roll. The blade's powerface is always loaded against the water. Initiate the move by leaning the canoe onside, touching the rail to the water. With your control hand chin high and shaft hand choked up, plant the blade in the water several feet away from the boat (Photo 53). Turning the control thumb in orients the powerface forward.

Sweep the paddle toward the bow and push against the water with the powerface. As the blade nears the bow, palm roll the control thumb down.

Draw the blade to the bow and complete a deep arc under the canoe (Photo 54), still pushing the water with the powerface. As the paddle passes back out from under the boat and is pushing away from the stern, your control thumb points down. Another palm roll orients the thumb away from the canoe and the paddle is ready for another cycle.

A reverse outer gimbal is used to rotate the stern toward the onside. It is based on the reverse palm roll, and as the blade traverses the underwater circle, the backface pushes against the water. Again, the paddle is held in a high brace position with the shaft nearly vertical. Bent shafts are inverted.

Photo 53: The Outer Gimble

Photos 54

Post/Christie Combination

Combining the quick, carving post with the stately, low brace christie results in a thrilling move. Exciting to perform, it's visually breathtaking and includes a fluid heel change in mid-maneuver. It's a great move for eddy turns in slow current.

From forward travel, initiate with a deep turning C or a cross forward to start the canoe turning onside while heeling the outside rail to the water. As the paddle clears the water during a horizontal recovery, plant a duffek over the high onside rail. There's our post—ride it.

When the rotation from the post slows, begin a deliberate bow draw and cross heel the canoe from offside to onside. Keep the torso vertical, unweighting the offside knee and smoothly transferring weight to the onside one. Guide the paddle through a deep C stroke, tracking the blade well under the hull. Palm roll from the thumb-down correction to a low braced christie. If greater rotation is desired, link the christie to an axle with another palm roll. The key to these moves is the palm roll. It maintains powerface continuity and a secure brace through the linked sequence.

Why link two maneuvers when either will generate the same rotation? How about for speed and stability. We're power linking two turns rather than riding one through. Ever misjudged a slow eddy? You post into it when the current isn't strong enough to pop you all the way around. Changing the lean and smoothly concluding the brace with a deep C should bring the hull in line. The continuation into a christie finishes the eddy turn.

Tandem Freestyle Moves

Tandem freestyle paddling is the logical and exciting extension of the solo work done in the seventies and eighties. Sport tandem canoes are short, lightweight and gently chined pocket cruisers that are fun to paddle. The extension of skidded freestyle maneuvers to tandem canoes adds the extra dimensions of team interaction and increased power to freestyle fun. With a paddler in each stem, the tandem canoe is more extensively controlled than a solo. One paddler moves the canoe into a turn, the second paddler provides continuing power or rotational enhancement. This extends the speed and rotation of maneuvers beyond a solo paddler's abilities.

Tandem maneuvers share the initiation, execution, and conclusion components of solo moves. As in solo, the leading stem is drawn, pryed or swept to one side and the trailing stem skids around it. The leading paddler applies turning draws or jams as in solo freestyle but with the option of extending paddle placement farther from the hull as the second paddler counterbalances body extension across the rail. The trailing tandem paddler helps balance the heel and has a variety of options: powering through the turn, enhancing the skid with reverse sweeps, or increasing stem lift by a weight shift. A tandem pair can achieve solid 180° turns on these maneuvers from a dead stop.

The tandem dynamic adds complexity and opportunity to canoeing, yielding greater rewards through synergistic interaction. A fair amount of interactive stick time may be appropriate before slamming the rail to the soup for a hot reverse move, but the work is fun. Freestyle tandem is exciting, self-expressive and fun, all enhanced by the interaction between the paddling team. Tandem freestyle transforms every pond into a dance floor, every stream into an exciting run, and every lake into a playground.

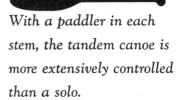

With a paddler in each stem, the tandem canoe is more extensively controlled than a solo.

The bow axle is the signature move of tandem freestyle paddlers.

Bow Axle

The bow axle is the signature move of tandem freestyle paddlers. With the hull heeled dramatically toward the bow's extended turning draw, the paddle planted several feet from the canoe, yet mystically supporting her weight, the axle is breathtaking to watch and exciting to play with.

Traveling forward, the bow initiates the bow axle with a drawing component to a forward stroke. Reading the draw, the stern helps initiate the move with a quarter sweep (Photo 55). This starts the canoe turning onside. Next, the bow rotates her torso onside, heeling the canoe down while planting a turning high brace abeam her hip and as far from the canoe as possible (Photo 56). Note: Her shaft arm is straight and the powerface is pitched at a thirty-degree angle of attack. Water pushes on the powerface, bracing the bow's extension and pulling the bow into the turn.

Maintain the heel, the inside rail flush to the water, through the maneuver, freeing the stems and reducing turning resistance. Unsteady bobbling causes turbulence and slows forward momentum. The stern, with broader knee placement and better vision of the relation between the water and the rail, holds the rail to the water while the stern skids around the bow's duffek. He sweeps through the turn (Photo 57), maintaining the original cadence.

As the turn loses momentum and slows, the bow opens her powerface to a more aggressive angle and slides it forward. From this extended position, she heels the boat upright and concludes the move with a draw to the bow followed by a forward stroke.

Touring, the bow plants the duffek and heels the canoe towards it, initiating the axle when a course correction is desired and trusting the stern to read her move and respond by sweeping the canoe through the intended turn. For play on the pond, where greater skid angles are desired, the bow

Photo 55: The bow axle

announces the axle to her stern with a countdown, enabling him to initiate the turn with a sweep while she adds a bow draw to her last forward stroke. She accentuates her extension across the rail, often hooking her offside calf under the seat to plant the paddle farther out and aft of her position. She extends the brace's duration by slowly moving the paddle forward, increasing blade angle and flotation. Turns of 180° are easy, with rotations past 360° possible.

An interesting axle variation has the stern paddler weighting forward in a feathered high brace rather than sweeping through the maneuver. A pure skid with the power off, the graceful precision required provides an indication of paddler finesse. It's a show move proving that the tandem team has the right stuff.

After a strong, initiating quarter sweep, the stern slices into a feathered high brace across the high rail of the canoe while weighting forward onto both

The axle is breathtaking to watch and exciting to play with.

Photo 56

Photo 57

knees. Or even better, he shifts to a high kneel. The stern may look neat, but the paddle is feathered to the skid. His sole contribution to the event is maintaining a firm heel while smoothly weighting forward to lift the stern high for a wilder skid. The stern concludes with a powerful quarter sweep from his extended, braced position as the bow heels the canoe upright.

Bow Post

When a canoe is heeled to the rail, it will turn away from the heel, so outside heeled turns will skid faster than inside heeled ones. The bow's deflection inside a heel is due to hydrodynamics, not pure black magic, and is the basis of all post turns. A post is identical to an axle except the canoe is leaned away from the side the paddle is planted. The post is an onside turn combining an onside turning draw with an outside heel. Good posture, with a vertical torso and a loose waist, help maintain balance. Weighting forward drives the bow deeper, enhancing its deflection into the maneuver while lifting the stern higher to further reduce resistance.

The post is an onside turn combining an onside turning draw with an outside heel.

The usual post includes the stern powering the canoe into the skid with a series of sweeps, as diagrammed in Figure 26 and illustrated in Photo 58. It is used while cruising whenever a quick onside turn is required to elude a turtle or catch an eddy, but let's describe the advanced variation with a stern high brace.

Visually compelling, with both paddlers across their respective rails in extended high braces, it is often called the double post. The name is misleading. While the bow's duffek pulls her stem into the move, the stern's duffek is feathered to the skid in an unloaded slice to a forward stroke. The bow starts heeling the canoe away from her paddle, starting the bow carving onside. The stern, noticing the bow's initiation, responds with a quarter sweep, breaking the stern into a skid towards his paddle.

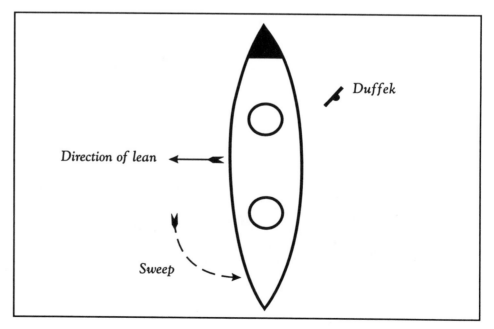

Figure 26: The bow post

Photo 58: The bow post

Photo 59

The bow recovers, planting a turning high brace or duffek and the stern slices to a feathered high brace. As the blades are planted, both paddlers continue heeling the canoe away from the turn until the offside rail touches the water.

Both paddlers shift their weight forward, burying the bow to enhance its deflection into the turn and increase the stern's lift, which in turn extends the skid by lowering stern turning resistance. Then the boat finishes the turn, while the paddlers carefully maintain the balance and steadiness of heel.

In conclusion, the canoe is heeled upright while the bow paddler draws to the bow and links to a forward stroke and the stern paddler performs a quarter sweep from his high brace placement. Both return their weight to their seats and continue with forward strokes.

Bow Wedge

The bow wedge is an unbraced offside maneuver away from the bow paddler's onside jam. It requires linking several facets for smooth effectiveness.

Traveling forward, the bow initiates the wedge with a quarter sweep while heeling the onside rail to the water. The outside heel starts the bow carving

The bow wedge requires linking several facets for smooth effectiveness.

Photo 60: The bow wedge

Photo 61

The turn is enhanced by using bent shafts and the execution of the bow's inverted jam.

inside the turn. The stern stabilizes the heel and helps initiate the move with a hard thumb-down forward hook. From horizontal recovery, the bow slices her blade forward, planting an inverted jam near her onside knee. The powerface is loaded at a closing angle of attack, pushing the blade toward the boat and turning the bow offside.

The stern paddler palm rolls from the hook to an inverted reverse sweeping low brace (or christie). The control thumb points forward and the blade's powerface addresses the water. The christie pushes the stern into a faster skid, enhancing the move's effectiveness. The paddlers maintain these positions, riding the skid.

As the skid slows, the bow paddler finishes with a sweep as the stern palm rolls into another hook. The turn is enhanced by using bent shafts and the execution of the bow's inverted jam (a backface-out jam is acceptable). The bow palm rolls to the concluding sweep. The bow's forward weight shift frees the stern and anchors the bow, increasing bow deflection into the move and lifting the stern for a wild skid. For the stern paddler, subtle linkage from the hook to a slow christie is key to a perfect maneuver.

The stern may choose to experiment with a feathered cross high brace. It's an extreme position, giving up the ability to power the skid and counterbalance an unbraced bow paddler, but it's fun to play with on warm, flat water.

Bow Cross Axle

Offside turns, away from the bow's paddle side, are always snappy, and the cross axle, with the canoe heeled to the opposite rail, towards the bow's cross duffek, is wild and abrupt. The cross axle is a good steerage move, giving the bow a tight offside turn away from obstacles, but it is also a great eddy move and useful in turning the hull parallel to shore for landing.

The cross axle is a good steerage move, but is also a great eddy move.

As an offside turn, the cross axle is initiated with the bow's powerful quarter sweep, which moves the canoe into the turn with increased headway. The stern, reading the bow's initiation, sets up with an exaggerated hooking correction to his forward stroke. The combination drives the canoe into the turn with power.

As the bow recovers, she carries the feathered blade across the bow to the offside with torso rotation aligning her shoulders to the keelline (Photo 62). Elevating her control hand and planting the blade at a thirty-degree opening angle of attack, the bow paddler draws the canoe bow inside the turn and towards her turning high brace. Her control thumb points away from the bow and towards the direction of the turn, and the shaft is almost vertical in the water (Photo 63). Generally, the bow shifts her weight forward onto her knees, extending her reach and pitching the hull down while heeling the canoe towards her paddle to free the stems.

The stern paddler helps heel the canoe down to the inside rail and drives the canoe through a medium angle turn with successive hook strokes. He drops his control thumb and over corrects each forward stroke. The canoe is set up to skid. However, this isn't as dynamic a turn as it could be.

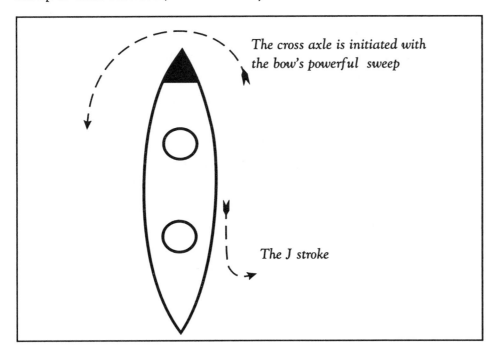

The cross axle is initiated with the bow's powerful sweep

The J stroke

Figure 27: The Bow Cross Axle

Photo 62: The bow cross axle

Photo 63

Both versions of the bow cross axle allow the stern paddler to enhance the stern's skid around the bow.

A reverse sweeping low brace is the answer, and this can be achieved in two ways, loading either powerface. From the conclusion of his thumb-down hooked initiation, the stern can flip the thumb back up, presenting the backface for a reverse sweeping low brace. Alternatively, the paddler can palm roll from the thumb-down position, inverting the paddle to load the powerface for an inverted reverse sweeping low brace or christie (Figure 28).

Both versions allow the stern paddler to enhance the stern's skid around the bow, creating a wilder skid. With straight paddles, the sole advantage of the palm roll is maintaining a brace in transition. With bents, inversion presents the powerface to the water for a more powerful reverse sweep and a flatter, ideally angled low brace.

The bow rides the move, perhaps choking up to reach out and presenting the paddle at a flatter angle for a better brace. Rotating her control thumb to open the blade maintains drawing force on the powerface. But when the impulse from the stern's reverse sweep fades, the bow slices her paddle out

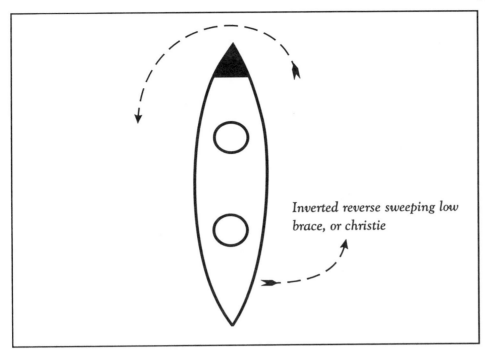

Inverted reverse sweeping low brace, or christie

Figure 28: A variation on the bow cross axle

before concluding the turn with a powerful, torso driven, cross bow sweep. If canoe seating won't allow the bow paddler to sweep across the bow, the paddle is cross drawn to the rail, lifted across the bow, and reinserted for a concluding quarter sweep before the canoe is heeled upright and both paddlers recover to forward strokes.

Paddlers will easily achieve 180° turns with the reverse sweeping low brace, but extreme angles of rotation require finesse. One trick is to think of the cross axle as a timing problem. The bow's plant of the high brace, the stern's reverse sweep, and the bow's cross bow draw must be spaced out to keep rotational force on the hull for as long as possible. Practice finds sympatico teams able to skid tandems past 270° without headway. Initiate and execute sloooowly, feeling each rotational force fade before starting the next, and conclude decisively. Who needs forward motion?

Paddlers will easily achieve 180° turns with the reverse sweeping low brace.

An exhibition variation of the cross axle is created when the stern executes a feathered cross high brace while maintaining the inside heel. This might be called a double cross axle except the stern paddler is not turning the canoe towards his high brace. High kneeling the move makes it look fancier, and the stern is ideally positioned for a cross sweeping conclusion. But the reverse sweep, which kicks the stern into a wild skid, is missing and is replaced by a pose that merely positions the stern to conclude nicely. This may not be the variation for windy days when you need to stick a 270.

Bow Cross Post

Canoes tend to carve turns away from heels. This is caused by differential deflection. The outside bow plane is presented to the water at a broad angle, while the inside bow plane becomes finer as the canoe heels. The canoe

Photo 64: The bow cross post

deflects into the turn just as a wood chisel digs in when driven upside down. Outside heeled turns are generally tighter than inside heeled ones, but the bow's cross post is an exception. Not as tight as its inside heeled cousin, the cross axle, the cross post is still a snappy maneuver, equally at home for obstacle avoidance, eddy moves and having fun.

As the maneuver is to the bow's offside, she initiates it with a powerful quarter sweep, actually accelerating into the maneuver. She heels the hull towards her paddle and away from the turn during the setup (Photo 65). The stern, noticing her initiation, sets a hard hooking correction on his forward stroke. The canoe should now be turning offside with power.

To set the turning high brace, the bow rotates her torso offside, aligning her shoulders with the keelline as she swings the feathered paddle across the bow. Without switching hand positions, she elevates her control hand and plants a turning high brace. The shaft is oriented vertically across the high offside rail, and the blade is pitched to a forty-degree opening angle of attack.

The stern weights his outside knee and lifts the inside one in order to help heel the outside rail right down to the soup. He may match his bow's lead with several stroke variations. He can drive the boat through a medium turn by continuing with a series of hooked forward strokes. But that's like work, especially over the high inside rail! Remembering that the stern wants to skid outside the carved path, let's encourage it with a reverse sweep.

The easiest way to kick the stern into a wild skidding ride is with a reverse sweeping low brace.

The easiest way to kick the stern into a wild skidding ride around the carving bow is with a reverse sweeping low brace loading the paddle's backface. After the thumb-down hook, the stern flips the thumb back to the horizontal, pointing abeam, and executes a reverse sweep with the blade flattened to provide some low brace component. Because the bent paddle's backface is somewhat ineffective for both power and bracing applications, let's try another option.

Photo 65: The bow cross post

If the stern palm rolls to a christie, he'll be using the more effective inverted reverse sweep and have the paddle oriented powerface down for optimal bracing affect. From his thumb-down hooking initiation, the stern loosens his control hand while pushing the loose shaft hand outwards, inducing the blade to roll over almost flat on the water. The control hand kneads across the grip in a smooth palm roll, leaving the control thumb pointed abeam.

While the bow rides her turning high brace, rotating the powerface to increasingly aggressive angles and slicing out to maintain both drawing and bracing forces on her powerface. The stern slooowly eases through his inverted reverse sweeping low brace.

When the christie is finished and rotational momentum fades, it's time to conclude the maneuver. Having sliced as far abeam as she can reach over the high offside rail, the bow paddler torso powers a dynamic cross bow sweep. The stern can ride the end position of his reverse quarter sweep, or if more secure of his balance, he can slice back to the hull for one final hook. Both paddlers then resume forward strokes or transition to reverse steerage.

A final variation—the fancy-looking stern cross high brace—can be attempted when the tandem team has the interactive timing perfected on initiation, heel and conclusion. Often nicknamed the double cross post, this is a wild looking move, where both paddlers high-hand their cross braces (Photo 66).

The stern weights forward from his initiating hook, planting a feathered cross high brace, remembering that any loading on either paddleface slows the skid. The advantage of this variation lies in the conclusion where the stern can power the hull farther into the carved turn with a powerful cross sweep.

The double cross post is a wild looking move, where both paddlers high-hand their cross braces.

Photo 66:
The double-cross post

The bow cross wedge is useful when an extremely tight turn is required.

Bow Cross Wedge

The bow cross wedge is a radical onside turn. It's useful when an extremely tight turn is required or when the stern paddler craves a wild ride.

From forward travel, the bow initiates the turn with a diagonal draw, while the stern executes a quarter sweep (Photo 67). The canoe is heeled onside and the boat starts carving to the bow's onside. After horizontal recovery, the bow swings the blade across the boat and palm rolls her control hand around the grip. Carrying the blade behind her hip, she slices it forward, powerface out, and intersects the hull and rail at her knee with a closing angle of attack. The bow deflects away from this inverted jam farther into the turn.

Photo 67:
The bow cross wedge

Photo 68

As the turn slows, the bow paddler opens her blade angle, increasing the inside deflection until momentum loss dictates a cross bow quarter sweep (Photo 68) to continue bow movement into the turn. As the sweep ends, the bow can use a horizontal recovery back onside or a feathered cross bow slice to a concluding onside draw. Weighting forward aids the entire maneuver by increasing the bow's bite and lifting the stern.

The stern's skid is enhanced by quarter sweeps over the outside rail. Or, the stern may weight forward from his initiating sweep, planting a feathered high brace. This is certainly more fun than sweeping. It provides a better chance of a significant brace and enhances the skid for a wilder ride.

Stern Axle

The stern axle is an efficient and elegant technique for turning a reversing canoe to the stern paddler's onside. With the boat leaned to the stern's onside, the maneuver pulls the canoe through a quiet arc—not abrupt, not harsh. Couple the axle with a series of bow reverse sweeps and the canoe is driven through the turn.

Couple the axle with a series of bow reverse sweeps and the canoe is driven through the turn.

The purpose of this move is to rotate the reversing canoe to the bow's offside. It is initiated with a bow reverse quarter sweep and a simultaneous stern draw. This initiation starts the stern turning towards the stern's paddle.

While the bow continues with reverse quarter sweeps, the canoe is heeled inside the turn towards the stern's paddle. The stern plants a reverse duffek abeam his hip. This is shown in Photo 69. The control thumb points towards the stern and away from the boat. Water pressure loads the powerface of the blade, pulling it away from the canoe.

The paddlers maintain this motion through the entire turn. The stern hangs out on a turning draw and the bow drives the canoe with reverse quarter

Photo 69: The bow is feathering a high brace during a stern axle.

sweeps. The heel is held constant and the inside rail is almost flush with the water. The maneuver concludes with the bow continuing reverse quarter sweeps and the stern executing a draw with the control thumb continuing to point toward the stern.

When the paddle nears the canoe, the stern paddler rotates it so the control thumb points away from the canoe. Then both paddlers heel the canoe level, link their last moves with back strokes, and accelerate out of the maneuver. As in all reverse maneuvers, the paddlers may also link to forward strokes.

With enough entry speed and a strong reverse quarter sweep by the bow paddler, the canoe can easily be driven through several rotations. However, if the inside lean is not maintained and the canoe bobbles or if the stern sets too aggressive an angle of attack with his paddle, the hull will lose speed. For an interesting and challenging variation, the bow can feather a high brace, counting on momentum to skid the hull around the stern's plant by virtue of a smooth heel.

Stern Post

While primarily a fun move, the reverse post can prove useful as an eddy move.

The stern post is a reversing carved move toward the stern's reverse duffek. The canoe is heeled outside the turn, allowing the wedge-shaped entry to offset the stern to the inside. While primarily a fun move, the reverse post can prove useful as an eddy move after running a riffle backwards.

From reverse travel, the move is initiated by the bow's reverse quarter sweep and the stern's drawing back stroke. The stern leans the canoe to the outside of the move while planting a reverse static draw. The powerface will be at an opening angle of attack and the water forces will pull it away from the boat. The bow's reverse quarter sweeps power the canoe through the needed angle of turn. The maneuver concludes with bow and stern draws as the canoe is rolled upright.

This move is limited in contrast to the forward post as the stern paddler cannot easily continue drawing forces on his stem as the turn loses momentum. The maximum torso rotation used in planting the static draw precludes the slicing motion that would expand it to a duffek. Nonetheless, adequate reverse headway and careful control of an extreme lean allows more fanciful variations. A finesse variation that features a bow's reverse feathered high brace offers the bow a wild swing around the stern's reverse duffek.

Stern Wedge

This sequence is a dynamic and stunning freestyle maneuver. Primarily used to quickly turn a reverse traveling boat to onside, it is also the initial segment of a striking reversal move. The maneuver is initiated with a stern reverse quarter sweep and a bow inverted back stroke with a hooked correction, as illustrated in Photo 70.

The boat is heeled onside and the stern executes a half palm roll and plants an inverted jam. The backface is against the canoe, and the powerface is loaded against the water (backface out and loaded jam if desired). At the same time, the bow palm rolls her paddle through a reverse hook until the powerface is flat on the water and her control thumb points outwards.

The paddlers hold these positions and let the canoe finish the maneuver. As illustrated in Photo 71, the bow can lean out a small amount on the paddle because it is in a low angled high brace. As the canoe turns towards the stern's offside, it will slow and the bow's brace will lose its effectiveness. The bow concludes with a slow quarter sweep while the stern performs an inverted reverse quarter sweep, loading the powerface while heeling the canoe level.

To recover, the stern slices the paddle from the water, performs the second half of a palm roll, and continues with back strokes. The bow slices in from her quarter sweep to back strokes as the canoe accelerates out of the turn in reverse. Alternatively, the paddlers may link to forward strokes,

Photo 70: The stern wedge

Photo 71: The stern wedge

The conclusion is quite powerful and capable of turning a heeled tandem past 90° by itself.

affecting a reversal of direction. In conditions where power is needed to complete the stern wedge, the bow may drive the canoe through the maneuver with a series of inverted hooked back strokes.

The bow may also use a feathered high brace, demonstrating that momentum and the stern's carving deflection into the move are sufficient to complete the maneuver. After initiation, the bow twists offside, swinging her paddle across the bow and planting a feathered cross high brace. After riding the maneuver, the bow concludes with a cross reverse quarter sweep, continuing across the bow for a recovery onside. This conclusion is quite powerful and capable of turning a heeled tandem past 90° by itself.

An alternate recovery sequence can be used to form a spectacular reversal move. The bow slices the blade from the water and swings it across the boat, or plants a cross duffek. At the same time, the canoe is leaned in the same direction and the stern half palm rolls and links to a reverse quarter sweep.

As the stern reverse sweeps, the bow cross draws and sweeps the blade past the front of the boat. The bow paddler may have to lean forward to get the blade past the boat. If this is physically impossible, the canoeist should simply cross draw to the bow and swing the blade over the canoe.

Now, the bow person links with a quarter sweep while the stern slices the blade to the canoe and links with a power stroke. The maneuver is concluded as the boat is leaned upright and both paddlers continue with forward strokes to accelerate the canoe forward.

With enough reverse entry speed and consistent lean (no bobbling), this maneuver can rotate the canoe through very large angles—maybe over 360°. Patience pays during this move. Let the boat turn on its own, using momentum and the stationary strokes to their fullest. Resist the urge to rush into the dynamic strokes.

Stern Cross Axle

Here's a wild looking but very controlled tandem move. It's a skidded turn to the bow paddler's onside with the stern planted and drawn inside by a cross duffek. The canoe is leaned toward the plant, lifting the stems to reduce turning resistance. The bow paddler powers through the move with a reverse christie. With both paddlers in a high brace off the same side of the canoe, it's a dramatic move that turns the hull 180°.

With the canoe running in reverse and both paddlers in cadence, the turn is initiated with a stern reverse sweep and a bow reverse turning C. This starts the hull turning away from the stern's paddle. The stern then plants a cross duffek while leaning the boat toward the paddle. The inside rail is right down to the water. The brace is a little tricky. Open the blade forty-five degrees to the keeline and place it as far off the rail and as far amidships as possible.

The bow can continue to reverse hook through the turn, but that is strenuous and drives the hull forward rather than accentuating the skid. A slow low bracing sweep is an improvement, but a reverse christie is the best. The bow paddler has turned her bent shaft paddle over during the reverse straight using the powerface with the offset grip backwards. Off her initiating reverse hook, she palm rolls her control hand in and up, maintaining force

The stern cross axle is a dramatic move that turns the hull 180°.

Photo 72: The Stern Cross Axle

Photo 73

on the powerface as the hook is linked to a low bracing quarter sweep. Accentuating the move, she may choke up on the shaft, increasing extension by slipping the shaft hand up.

As the sweep moves off the bow, the paddle is rolled further over to a knuckles-up configuration that is a low-angled high brace. As the sweep continues, the shaft hand is slipped back down. The bow paddler extends over the inside rail, her offside calf hooked under the seat to increase extension. To finish the turn, the stern paddler sweeps toward the rear and links to a concluding draw while rolling the boat upright.

The bow paddler feathers her brace amidships as the hull rights and then palm rolls, maintaining proper powerface, into a slow outward pry before concluding with a sweep and horizontally recovering to a forward stroke. Now, the canoe has been turned completely around with a lot of drama and is running in the original direction. Nifty and wild looking.

Stern Cross Post

The reversing stern cross post is a stately maneuver usually performed with the bow paddler extended in a reversing feathered cross high brace. The stern initiates with a sweeping back stroke, the bow initiates with a hooking back stroke. The canoe is heeled offside away from the maneuver. The stern paddler's carving deflection into the move is as important to the maneuver as his reverse cross duffek. The bow paddler's feathered cross duffek provides a marginal option for a brace, but more importantly, it positions her to help maintain the heel and to deliver a powerful cross reverse quarter sweep all the way across her bow. While a fine move for dusk on a still city park pond, the stern cross post isn't popular on tours.

Stern Cross Wedge

By way of paraphrasing a well-worn quotation, it might be said that "the stern cross wedge was executed because it was there." It is a carving offside turn practiced to prove a point. It demonstrates an advanced knowledge of canoe hydraulics and precise hull control, but is not likely to be used far from the confines of the city park pond.

The stern cross wedge demonstrates an advanced knowledge of canoe hydraulics and precise hull control.

From reverse headway, the stern initiates the maneuver with a reverse diagonal draw and the bow uses a reverse sweep. Then the stern leans the hull to the outside of the turn while crossing the hull and palm rolling the paddle). Using maximum torso rotation, the stern slices a powerface-out inverted jam to the rail behind his offside hip. The blade intersects the hull at a closing angle of attack. (Try substituting a backface-out jam.) The stern holds on and rides out this radical unbraced maneuver.

The bow paddler enhances the wild skid with successive reverse sweeps or reverse sculling sweeps. When the inward stern deflection slackens, the stern levers his paddle through a cross reverse quarter sweep from the wedge

Photo 74:
The stern cross wedge

Photo 75: The stern axle

before uprighting the hull and recovering onside or linking to another reverse move. (Try linking to a reverse stern axle.)

Maintaining extreme heel while reverse sweeping convinces most bows that they could do something else to improve enjoyment of the maneuver. Try a feathered high brace, which offers a saving brace should things go awry and improves visual presentation.

Linking Tandem Maneuvers

Smoothly linking one maneuver to another is fun, a great demonstration of advancing paddling skills, and a bio-kenetic high. The concept is to have the maneuvers practiced to the point that they can be achieved cleanly without headway. To link one maneuver to another, we conclude so the paddle is in position to initiate the successive move.

The potential combinations are extensive, but let's start with a proven linkage of four maneuvers. A pleasing series of skidded spins can be performed by linking the cross wedge, the stern axle, the axle, and the wedge.

The cross wedge skids the canoe onside with an outside heel away from the spin. The stern concludes with a draw from an extended high brace and slices right back out into a reverse duffek while maintaining the heel. The bow

A pleasing series of skidded spins can be performed by linking the cross wedge, the stern axle, the axle, and the wedge.

paddler concludes with a cross sweep and slices around the bow, driving the hull through the stern axle with a series of reverse quarter sweeps.

When tired of the stern axle, the bow opens her powerface into a turning high brace from the catch position for another reverse sweep as the stern concludes the reverse move with a draw from his reverse high brace. Both partners cross heel the canoe and the stern paddler quarter sweeps them through the desired rotation. (And that can be several full rotations.)

The bow then sweeps from her duffek while the stern hooks a forward stroke from his last sweep. The bow slices into her jam while the stern hooks through the wedge, maybe crossing for a feathered high brace and a cross drawing conclusion to the wedge.

This combo won't get a canoe down Lake Agnes quickly, but it will get the team across the park pond with style. And, it's creative fun to link maneuvers. Whether in the city park on a Sunday or with the loons after supper on the canoe trail, have fun!

Part IV: Paddling Competition
Or "The Games People Play."

Judged Freestyle Competitions

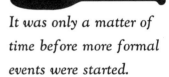

It was only a matter of time before more formal events were started.

Watch a freestyle enthusiast on a day tour and what do you see? At every opportunity—lunch break, rest stop, etc.—the paddler stops to play, trying new strokes or enjoying old moves. Put two freestyle enthusiasts together on a small lake and what happens? Instant dueling canoes, each paddler trying to out do the other. With all this friendly competition going on, it was only a matter of time before more formal events were started.

Interpretive freestyle began to take competitive form in 1988. Mike Galt had been performing paddling exhibitions for over a year. Then, at Conclave '88 in Champaign, Illinois, he tried an experiment. Selecting bow paddlers from the crowd, he put on short, spontaneous paddling programs. It was an exciting moment for tandem freestyle paddling, and lots of fun.

Later that spring, while watching Mike perform the same program at L.L. Bean's Canoe Symposium in Maine, a red-headed magazine publisher suggested that we might try paddling to music like the figure skater's long program. After six months of meetings, phone calls, and rule revisions, freestylers had a pilot Interpretive Paddling Competition ready for Conclave 1989. It was a hit, with several thousand spectators enjoying the first-ever event. Since then, the rules have undergone numerous revisions, and by the summer of 1990, enough spectator and competitor interest had developed for the ACA's Recreation Committee to endorse national competitions.

Currently, there are two judged events for freestyle paddlers. The Classic Figures Competition is similar to the school figures event of ice skating, while the Interpretive freestyle Competition is analogous to skating's long program. Both are administered by the ACA's Freestyle Committee and current rules are available from the ACA office in Springfield, VA.

Classic Figures Competition

Designed by Tom MacKenzie at the instigation of David Yost, the Classic Figures Competition was developed as both a training drill and a competitive event, judged by stringent technical standards. It is a judged freestyle contest for solo and tandem open canoes, during which competitors, using single-bladed paddles, must execute a series of precise turns on a two-buoy course. It is a paddling discipline and a paddling drill. Carving a 180° turn in freestyle form when and where you wish is one thing, but maneuvering around a fixed object, whether or not you're ready, and whether or not the wind, current, and hull position are cooperating is quite another. School figures sharpen technical skills in a format encouraging practice, just as musicians must practice their scales.

The Classic Figures is not a race and is not timed. Its seven-point scoring system rewards fine boat control and paddling finesse—a graceful progression through the turns. Judges look for smooth initiation and recovery. They score highly when the rail is leaned to the water throughout each turn, held there with no apparent strain or obvious effort. The canoe should appear to move effortlessly, guided by form, not force. In essence, the Classic Figures comprise the compulsory turns required in Interpretive Freestyle Competitions—without the music and choreography.

The canoe should appear to move effortlessly, guided by form, not force.

The Figures are an important component of the ACA's Freestyle Paddling Instructional Course. They are often used in conjunction with video taping to evaluate a paddler's progress. As such, Classic Figures are a valuable teaching tool and a source of paddling enjoyment; flexibility is part of the appeal. Include a figures course at club outings or toss a pair of buoys into the local pond to practice for your own satisfaction.

To run the event, you must set up a course. This requires two buoys, spaced sixty feet apart and positioned parallel to shore. Milk jugs anchored with bricks make fine buoys.

The participants pass through the course individually and follow a specified routine. Right-sided solo paddlers and bow right tandem teams begin to the right of the home buoy, bow in line with the buoy. Left-sided solo paddlers and bow left tandem teams start to the left of the home buoy.

1. Paddle to the second buoy and turn around it with an axle.
2. Return to the home buoy and turn around it with a cross axle.
3. Paddle to the second buoy and maneuver around it with a post.
4. Again, return to the home buoy and turn around it with a cross post.
5. Paddle to the second buoy and turn around it with a wedge. Stop, then exit the field in reverse, parallel to the line connecting the buoys.

The judging criteria are the same as the ones used for compulsory moves in Interpretive Freestyle Competition. A perfect maneuver scores seven points, and each of the five moves mentioned above is scored separately. A maximum

maximum of one point is subtracted for the failure of any of the following elements:

1. Initiation of turn—smooth and subtle.
2. Lean of canoe—rail to the water (no bobble).
3. Form—paddle and body positioning, fluid motion.
4. Symmetry—constant radius around buoy (don't touch it).
5. Degree of rotation—minimum 180° turn required (no extra strokes).
6. Synchrony—uniform cadence for solo paddler; matching strokes for a tandem team.
7. Conclusion—effective and subtle; includes finishing straightaway.

Interpretive Freestyle Competition

Interpretive Freestyle Competition is a time and space limited contest during which paddlers demonstrate precise control of the open canoe while creating a visually pleasing and artistic performance. Routines of five minutes maximum duration are usually choreographed to music and showcase technical paddling skills while providing an artistic interpretation of the music.

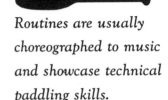

Routines are usually choreographed to music and showcase technical paddling skills.

The arena is limited to a fifty by thirty meter area, the long side parallel to shore. This helps keep routines tight and visually interesting for the audience. It also will allow future indoor competitions to be held in larger swimming pools without boundary adjustment.

A set number of compulsory turns are judged according to the same criteria used for Classic Figures competition. In addition, the routines in the Interpretive Freestyle Competition are also evaluated in four overall criteria: Technical Execution, Technical Difficulty, Choreography, and Showmanship.

1. Technical Execution includes effectiveness of strokes and maneuvers, smoothness, matching strokes and maintaining cadence, and effectiveness of initiations, leans and conclusions.
2. Technical Difficulty includes number of turns, angles of rotation, variety and difficulty of maneuvers, and variations attempted.
3. Choreography includes coordination of moves and cadence to music, musical interpretation, tightness of routine, linking of maneuvers, and smoothness of transitions.
4. Showmanship includes personal presentation, dynamic and dramatic qualities of routine, and ability to entertain audience.

Finale

Interpretive Freestyle is a crowd-pleasing, elegant, and expressive event. It is staggering to think that canoe paddling has become a spectator sport in just a few years. But, why not? Perhaps our national sport has come of age. The

Perhaps our national sport has come of age.

Routines can be stately and elegant or fast-paced and hot, but they all stimulate and provoke.

paddlers are practiced, and current technical standards, demanding linked 180° turns with minimal strokes between maneuvers, yields a tight, exciting program. Routines can be stately and elegant or fast-paced and hot, but they all stimulate and provoke. Exhibitions and competitions are watched, and they seem to be establishing new, visible standards of excellence in paddling skill.

But, how does one develop the self-confidence to perform before an audience of fifteen hundred people? Well, try starting with school figures and take a cassette tape player along for the ride. Just paddle to the music. The choreography will follow. Paddling to music, interpreting the flow with motion, is fun and offers private and public opportunities for self expression.

Giant Slalom
Introduction and History

The American Heritage Dictionary defines slalom as "skiing in a zigzag course" or "a race along such a course, laid out with flag-marked poles." The word, Norwegian in origin, was originally applied to alpine skiing and now encompasses all aspects of the sport, including giant slalom, and to a certain degree, downhill racing. Besides being fun, alpine slalom racing exercises the essential skills of skiing, the level depending on which event is being challenged. Slalom is also very exciting for the spectators—watching the racers fly down the slope, negotiating a series of closely-spaced, tight turns.

Water skiers also enjoy slalom events and so do some car racers, but this book is about canoeing, specifically freestyle canoeing, so it's canoe slalom we wish to present. The reader is probably already familiar with canoe slalom. The ACA, as well as other groups, hosts frequent competitions throughout the country and around the world. Until recently, these events were held exclusively on whitewater rivers, the competitors charging down short (maybe one-quarter mile) sections of waterway, negotiating closely-spaced gates hung from cables strung across the river. In another form of whitewater event called "downriver," the participants race over much larger distances, and even though there are no turn gates situated along the course, the paddlers must still precisely maneuver their craft through the natural obstructions.

Whitewater slalom and downriver events are challenging and fun. Canoe designers continue to create better competition boats, and these advancements eventually lead to improved recreational designs. The competitors? Well, inevitably their technique is dramatically refined and they learn effective turning, precise river reading, and efficient paddling—skills that transcend the racing and are directly applicable to everyday boating.

Competitors learn skills that transcend racing and are directly applicable to everday boating.

But slalom is not just for whitewater. Several years ago, the sport was introduced to the quietwater community and things have not been the same since. Perhaps the first acknowledged presentation of the event in quietwater circles occurred at the First (and only) Annual Canoe Expo held in Raleigh, North Carolina, in May of 1987. Harold Deal, a superb freestyle paddler and the 1983, '86, and '91 ACA Solo Combined Class Whitewater National Champion, had developed a challenging course and was invited to the Expo to feature this new activity. His layout was a pleasing mixture of tight turns, straights, and demanding reversal gates set up around an array of colorful buoys, cleverly crafted from the all-American plastic milk jug.

No formal competition was held. Instead, Harold demonstrated the event, easily moving through the course and displaying the benefits of precise boat handling skills. Later, the course was open to the public. That same year the Peninsula Paddling Club of Florida was formed. An ardent group of sport canoeists in the organization began instructing introductory level clinics in freestyle paddling and were looking for innovative teaching techniques. Slalom was a natural! The buoys made excellent turn markers and the paddlers quickly sharpened their skills. More importantly, it was fun!

The paddlers quickly sharpened their skills. More importantly, it was fun!

Soon, boaters began challenging one another to friendly races, and before long, slalom competition? became a regular event at the bimonthly club fun days. Several course layouts were developed. Different buoy designs were tried, and the milk jug was replaced by a more convenient and user-friendly marker. More on this later.

Another major milestone was achieved in June of 1988 when the club was invited to conduct the first-ever slalom races as part of the canoe competition for the Orlando Sports Festival (a regional event of the Florida Sunshine State Games). What an achievement! The freestyle canoeists mixed with the other paddlers and everyone enjoyed the camaraderie and challenge of racing through the buoys. The event was so successful that slalom racing has become a regular event in the Sports Festival.

But quietwater slalom really came of age in 1989 with the passage of two significant events. First, the general character of the course layouts was changed by increasing the average distance between gates. Previously the short, tight courses unfairly favored highly maneuverable canoes, and in fact, rockered whitewater boats frequently won the event. By increasing the distance between buoys this advantage was eliminated. A more equitable mix of paddling skills and canoe design was required as straight-ahead speed now became as important as maneuverability. Graceful, precise turning and efficient traveling power strokes were on a par, and effective overall boat handling was now emphasized. The name of the event was also changed to giant slalom to reflect the increased distances.

The second significant event of 1989 was Conclave, an on-water paddling event that brought together boaters from all over the country. This was the first time giant slalom was played at a national level. Competition and spectator response was electric. This was a visually thrilling event to watch and a physically exciting event to compete in. In fact, the response was so positive that giant slalom became an integral part of that show.

In 1990, the ACA became actively involved with promoting the freestyle paddling movement and giant slalom was accepted as one of the freestyle competitive events. Later that same year, the first ACA Giant Slalom National Championships were held at Conclave '90 Midwest.

Getting Started

Clubs and other groups of paddlers can easily initiate friendly giant slalom competition. All that's needed is a set of buoys, an interesting and challenging course layout, a body of water large enough to accommodate the course, a stopwatch, a short set of rules, and the appropriate canoes and paddles. Although some races are run as "one-design class" events (meaning a single solo design and tandem design are used), most sanctioned competitions are typically held as "run what you brung" races. Here, the objective is not necessarily beating the other entrants but rather running a fast time—in effect, competing against oneself.

The objective is not necessarily beating the other entrants but rather running a fast time.

Buoys

The first set of equipment needed for running a slalom event is a group of buoys. These floating markers are used to designate turning gates. A buoy consists of a numbered float, an anchor, and a line connecting the two. A very simple float can be made from a one gallon plastic milk jug (don't forget the top or else the float will sink) that can be colored with waterproof paint and numbered with a broad tip marker. The anchor line is attached to the milk jug with a knot tied around the jug handle.

Buoys should be colored to designate turning direction and indicate the side on which the marker should pass the canoe. For instance, a white buoy will designate a left turn and should pass the boat along the left rail. The opposite is true for a red buoy. The buoys should be numbered, of course, to indicate the order in which they are run.

A styrofoam ball (used for lobster and crab trap markers and fishing net floats) also makes a simple buoy float. These are attached to the anchor line with a knot tied above the hole that passes through the ball.

With the addition of a little more hardware, the styrofoam ball can be fashioned into a fancier and more functional float. Pass a wood dowel rod though the center hole and secure it with washers and cotter pins. Slide a small section of lead plumbing pipe onto the bottom of the dowel rod and secure it with a D-ring (usually found on backpacking equipment and available in most outdoor stores). The pipe serves to balance the float and keep it upright, while the D-ring is a convenient location to tie the anchor line. A numbered flag can be made from a waterproof vinyl material (available at many sign shops and used for outdoor banners and pennants). This material typically has a sewn sleeve that is useful for sliding over the dowel rod. Cut the flag to the desired shape and finish off with three-inch tall sticky back numerals (available at most office supply stores).

Anchors can be made from the three-hole bricks used for fireplace facades, although construction blocks will provide considerably more weight to hold the floats in place. The small, lightweight anchors used for hunting decoys also make effective moorings. The pointed flukes around the main body grip the sandy lake bottoms or snag in undergrowth and hold the assembly in place.

Course Layouts

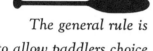

The general rule is to allow paddlers choice of direction at the turn-around buoy.

A simple out-and-back course can be designed with as few as six or seven buoys and a start/finish gate. This type of course will have eleven or thirteen turns and is guaranteed to be balanced with both right and left turns. The general rule is to allow paddlers choice of direction at the turn-around buoy. The major disadvantage with an out-and-back setup is the limitation on course utility—only one paddler may be on the loop at a time. This can slow an event down. A decided advantage of this type of course, though, is its usefulness on smaller ponds and other narrow waterways.

Naturally, looped courses allow multiple paddlers to be on the water simultaneously. Unfortunately, these setups require a larger area of water and this could effect the availability of useful sites. Also, looped courses are more difficult to design for balance between right- and left-handed paddlers.

A setup with twelve to fourteen gates is optimum because it allows the racers to work hard without pushing past the point of exhaustion. After all, the real purpose of giant slalom is to practice "boat handling." A good course should have an interesting variety of tight and gradual turns connected with straightaways that vary in length from thirty to seventy-five feet. A sharp (say 180°) turn after a long straight requires the paddler to quickly transfer the boat's forward momentum into the opposite direction while a "chicane" (a series of low-angle turns alternating left to right connected by short straights) requires the canoeist to accelerate through the turns—difficult at best. A "reverse gate" in the middle of a long straight is also a good test of more advanced paddling skills.

A balanced course has an equal number of left and right turns. It also has an equal number of tight turns to each side. The general rule is to develop a design that stresses the lefty as much as the righty.

Finally, for spectator appeal, the final straight should be a long one. This gives the crowd ample time to experience the excitement of the finish. It's also an additional test of the competitor's stamina and boat handling abilities—just try racing down a long straight when you're tired and your paddling finesse is quickly losing ground to muscle fatigue.

Rules

Keep it simple! Keep it fun! Minimize the number of rules you inflict on the participants. Don't penalize a racer for touching a buoy. Not only is it difficult to tell when contact has occurred, it also requires additional officials to police the course and look for infractions. You must, however, penalize for missing a gate. Adding thirty to forty-five seconds per missed buoy is typical and will deter anyone from deliberately skipping a gate in the pursuit of a fast time.

Keep it fun! Minimize the number of rules you inflict on the participants.

Finale

Giant slalom is an excellent tool for sharpening our boat handling skills. The desire to paddle hard and fast while maintaining precise control places a premium on developing good paddling technique. Full and constant boat leans and efficient strokes are all required. The fun of a little friendly competition amongst peers simply adds to the excitement.

Paddling Games

Paddlers are an exuberant bunch, so it is natural that impromptu games break out where paddlers gather. The two most popular informal contests played by freestylists are Dead Fish Polo and Tape Tag.

Dead Fish Polo

Dead Fish Polo originated in northern Minnesota in the late 1970's. While gliding across the glass-like border of a mystic lake, a paddler noticed a bulging, lifeless bluegill bobbing against a shock of wild rice. Concerned with preserving the pristine nature of the northern lake, our ardent tourer lifted the deceased from the waters with his paddle.

Having no proper place to deposit the defunct fish, he deftly dunked it into his paddling partner's Proem. Hence, Dead Fish Polo was born. The combative nature of the contest—a frantic attempt to resist possession of the prize—soon required that rules be formulated.

For the uninitiated, Dead Fish Polo is an elimination contest where the last remaining boat is declared the winner. The game is played in open canoes, paddled solo, and begins when a soggy sponge (symbolizing a dead fish) is tossed into the midst of a group of canoes. The objective is to maneuver your canoe adeptly to the vicinity of the sponge, lift the sponge out of the water using only the blade of your paddle, and then flip it into a fellow competitor's boat. Any paddler who allows a sponge to land in his or her canoe is eliminated and must leave the field of action. The sponge is returned to the water and action continues. More than one sponge may be put into play if there is a large number of competitors. The rules are simple and concise:

1. A wooden paddle is mandated to preserve the genteel nature of friendly competition. Paddles of other materials are specifically disallowed.

The combative nature of Dead Fish Polo required that rules be formulated.

2. Aluminum canoes and decked canoes are disallowed.

3. Switching hands on the paddle is not allowed. You must paddle with a designated control hand.

4. Excessive aggressive tactics, such as paddle bashing or boat ramming, are forbidden. This is not a destruction derby.

5. The standing rule is invoked for practicing either excessive aggression or conservative tactics.

6. Anyone who capsizes is eliminated.

Rule violators are eliminated and must leave the field of action. The standing rule is usually brought into play when only two or three competitors remain in the game and the action is starting to drag. The referee directs the remaining players to stand in their canoes, continuing the game in that position. Needless to say, the game usually comes to a prompt conclusion. Players who attempt to win by lurking around the fringes of the action or basing others are also asked to stand.

More seriously, Dead Fish Polo is an effective and fun way to develop solo paddling skills. It stresses speed, maneuverability, and balance in a competitive game that requires the paddler to concentrate on something other than boat handling skills. The strategy employed to elude those wet sponges removes much of the fear of failure that may be associated with learning to control a solo canoe. Strokes and maneuvers tend to come naturally as a paddler concentrates on escaping the sponge.

For a more challenging game, replace the sponges with rubber balls. They hold less water, are harder to pick up, balance on the paddle, and travel farther when thrown.

At its wildest, Tape Tag resembles the confused melee of a dogfight between fighter planes.

Tape Tag

Tape Tag is an energetic and exciting game that emphasizes precise boat handling. It is played in solo canoes, and at its wildest, resembles the confused melee of a dogfight between fighter planes.

To play, each contestant sticks a six-inch strip of duct tape to the bow and stern of his or her canoe. It is unfair to wrap the tape around grab thwarts. The object of the game is to maneuver close enough to an opposing paddler to remove the bow and/or stern tape strip. Of course, while maneuvering, you must protect your own tape from removal. When both of a player's tape strips have been removed, he or she is eliminated from the game.

Although the game is an elimination contest, the last remaining person is not necessarily the winner. That honor goes to the paddler who collected the most strips.

Glossary of Freestyle Terms

Abeam. 1.) Laterally perpendicular to keelline at amidships. 2.) A non-torquing lateral movement.

Amidships. Longitudinal midpoint between bow and stern.

Angle of Attack. The angle of the blade to the keelline; opening away from keelline or closing towards it.

Asymmetry. Dissimilarity of mirror image forms; hulls with the widest beam other than amidships, paddles with differing blade or grip faces.

Axle. An inside heeled skid around a turning draw.

Beam. The canoe's width.

Bilge. Hull transition area between bottom and sides, also chine.

Bow. Forward portion of hull where sides join.

Bow Jam. Paddle used as forward rudder, backface out at closing angle of attack; jams turn canoes away from the paddle.

Bow Wedge. A maneuver including an outside heel and a jam or inverted jam, turning the hull away from the paddle placement.

Brace. Force loading the blade to improve stability and prevent tipping (see low brace, high brace, and prying brace).

Broach. Sideways position across current or wave pattern.

C Stroke. Solo paddler's traveling stroke; links a controlling bow draw, a forward stroke, and a corrective stern pushaway; can be exaggerated into a turn towards the onside.

Carve. A deflected turn away from a heel, caused by differential entry angles and forces.

Catch. A stroke's beginning, the blade entering the water.

Center of Gravity. A point balancing gravitational forces.

Center of Lateral Resistance. Point balancing lateral forces.

Center of Rotation. Axis of the radius of a turn.

Chine. Intersection of the hulls vertical sides with its horizontal bottom.

Christie. An onside, inside heeled turn actuated by an inverted, reverse sweeping low brace, pushing stern into skid.

Conclusion. A move or moves finalizing a freestyle maneuver.

Control Hand. The hand gripping the paddle's top grip.

Control Stroke. A pitch or directional vector in frontal resistance that alters a stroke's effect on canoe movement.

Correction. A pitch or vector in eddy resistance, altering a stroke's effect on hull movement.

Cross Strokes. Strokes where the paddle is carried across the hull and placed offside without changing hand positions.

Cross Axle. A freestyle maneuver, the hull heeled to and turned towards a cross turning draw or duffek.

Cross Draw. An offside draw.

Cross Duffek. An offside turning draw, the blade placed at an opening attack angle.

Cross Heel. Heeling the hull away from the onside.

Cross Post. A freestyle maneuver, the hull heeled outside, away from a move around a cross duffek.

Cross Wedge. A freestyle maneuver, the hull heeled outside turn, hull turning away from jam or inverted jam.

Dedicated Powerface. A paddle having only one blade surface usable as powerface by shaft bend, asymmetrical grip, or blade shape.

Deflection. Forces causing a carved turn away from an outside heel by differential force loading on the bow planes.

Draw. A stroke pulling the canoe or stem sideways towards a paddle placement.

Duffek. A dynamic turning high brace, featuring an open angle of attack linking to a reverse sweep and a bow draw.

Dynamic. A moving stroke or maneuver, as contrasted to a static one.

Eddy Resistance. Turbulent resistance, or drag, on the trailing portion of the canoe behind the maximum beam.

Eddy Turn. Planting paddle or bow in differential current, eddy, allowing the moving current to snap the hull around.

Feather. Pitching, or flattening, the blade attack angle, reducing air or water resistance.

Ferry. Crossing a current with a diagonal, upstream hull angle and a downstream heel, creating vectors inhibiting downstream movement.

Final Stability. The amount of stability with the canoe heeled to the rail.

Flare. A hull cross-section widening from keel to rails.

Force Load. Applying force against a powerface.

Freeboard. The vertical distance from waterline to gunwale.

Freespin. A turn due solely to the differential stem deflection caused by heeling the canoe.

Freestyle. A paddling style emphasizing heeled, skidded turns.

Frontal resistance. Hull resistance to water before canoe beam.

Giant Slalom. A specific freestyle competition combining speed with turning ability on a buoyed course.

Gimbal. Linkage of high or low-braced sweeps or reverse sweeps, spinning a canoe through a full rotation.

Grip. Shaped, upper end of the paddle shaft, grasped by the control hand as the paddle's steering wheel.

Gunwales. Longitudinal reinforcements along top edges of the canoe hull.

Hanging Draw. A static draw, the paddle planted abeam at an opening angle of attack, creating vectors drawing the hull towards the placement.

Heel. Tipping the canoe to either side, changing hull shape, shortening wetted length, and lifting stem resistance.

High Brace. A brace placed at a high paddle angle, the blade feathered, control thumb pointed to rear, resisting tipping to either side.

High Kneel. A paddling stance with the paddler on one knee in onside chine, the opposite foot placed forward with knee high.

Horizontal Recovery. Paddle carried forward for successive stroke through the air, the shaft level and the blade feathered.

Hook. A corrective outward pry at the end of a forward stroke in drag resistance, countering the canoe's tendency to turn away from the paddle; also, a tip curvature towards a paddle's powerface.

Hull. The shaped outer surface of a canoe.

Initial Stability. A canoe's resistance to heeling or tipping from an upright position.

Initiation. A stroke or move beginning a freestyle maneuver.

Inner Gimbal. Linking forward or reverse sweeping low braces to spin the canoe; the paddle feathered to sweep under the hull.

Inside Heel. Heeling the hull towards the direction of turn.

Interpretive Freestyle. Choreographed paddling to music, also an ACA competition judging same.

Invert. Turning the paddle over, force loading the opposite face.

Inverted Jam. A jam with the powerface outwards and backface to the hull with the blade pitched to a closing angle of attack.

In-Water Recovery. Carrying the paddle forward for a successive stroke through the water; the blade is feathered, the shaft vertical and elevated.

Jam. The blade used as a canard; planted against or near the hull at a closing angle of attack, backface out (see inverted jam, pry and wedge).

J Lean. Heeling the canoe by pivoting the body at the pelvic girdle, keeping the torso erect.

J Stroke. A corrective forward stroke, using a strong pry conclusion to counter torque and keep the canoe on course (see hook and C strokes).

Keelline. The hull's longitudinal centerline.

Lateral Extension. Sideways extension parallel to keelline

Lean. Heeling, or tipping the canoe, laterally, changing in-water hull shape and dynamics.

Link. Smoothly melding strokes or moves, maintaining continuity of hull movement.

Longitudinal Buoyancy Center. The point balancing hull displacement fore to aft.

Low Brace. A brace with a low paddle angle, control thumb pointing forward, used to resist onside tips.

Maneuver. A combination of initiatory, executive, and conclusive strokes, heel, and weight shift, altering a canoe's movement.

Move. A maneuver (see maneuver).

Neck. The part of the paddle directly below the top grip.

Offset Grip. A paddle's top grip shaped to overhang the paddle's backface; generally dedicates a powerface on straight paddles.

Offside. The side of the canoe away from the selected paddle side (see onside).

Offside Turn. A turn away from the selected paddle side.

Onside. The selected paddleside of the canoe, as contrasted to offside, where cross strokes would be placed.

Onside Heel. A heel towards selected paddle side.

Onside Turn. A turn towards selected paddle side.

Outside Lean. Heeling hull away from the direction of turn.

Outer (High Brace) Gimbal. Palm roll linking duffek, bow draw, turning C, and stern pry, spinning hull past 360°.

Paddle side. The selected side of canoe, where the paddle and shaft hand occur for normal (not cross) strokes.

Palm Roll. Changing control hand position on the top grip, altering grip orientation to maintain powerface continuity.

Peel Out. Entering moving water from an eddy (see eddy turn) by moving the bow or paddle across the eddy line into downstream current; lean downstream to resist capsize.

Pitch (paddle). A variation of blade angle from 90° to direction of paddle movement, introducing drawing or prying vectors.

Pitch (hull). Forward or aft paddler weight shift, affecting trim.

Pitch Stroke. Angling the blade during a stroke, introducing control or corrective force vectors to the stroke.

Post. A duffek actuated turn, the hull heeled outside, away from the turn, starting the stems carving.

Powerface. The side of the blade loaded against the water (see backface).

Propulsion. Causing canoe movement by applying force to water through the blade.

Pry. Forcing the hull sideways, away from paddle placement by levering the blade out off the rail.

Prying Brace. Slicing the paddle to the rail and prying to resist an offside capsize.

Pry. Pushing the paddle out from the rail, powerface out, to move sideways or abeam, away from the paddle placement.

Quarter Sweep. A 90° sweeping stroke from bow to amidships or amidships to stern.

Rake. Overhanging rather than plumb stems.

Recovery. Returning the paddle to catch position (see horizontal recovery, in-water recovery, and catch).

Reserve Stability. The hull's resistance to capsize when heeled.

Reverse Stroke. Paddle movement from the stern towards the bow.

Reverse Combination. Linking a christie to an axle.

Rib. Reinforcing ridges on blades and in canoes hulls.

Rocker. Upward curvature of a canoe keel at the stems.

Rotate. A spin or stationary turn, both ends revolving around axis at center of buoyancy.

Rotational Center. The point about which a hull spins or turns.

Rudder. A static, pitched paddle placement at a canoe's stem.

Scull. Reciprocating longitudinal stroke, with the blade pitched and force loaded to cause drawing or pushing forces.

Shaft. The paddle section connecting the blade and top grip.

Shaft Hand. The hand gripping the paddle shaft; the lower hand.

Sheer. Longitudinal curvature of the canoe's top edge.

Shift. A lateral, non-torquing canoe movement (see sideslip).

Shoulder Plane. The plane formed by both shoulders and the paddler's belt buckle; arm extension behind shoulder plane risks shoulder dislocation.

Side of Opposition. The side of the canoe opposing abeam movement.

Sideslip. A lateral movement, without torque, of a canoe moving forward or in reverse (see abeam).

Skid. An accelerating turn; one stem spinning around the other.

Slice. A feathered, in-water, paddle movement.

Snap Turn. A reverse sweeping low brace, loading the backface.

Spin. Stems rotating around the rotational center at equal rates.

Spine. Lengthwise rib down the longitudinal center of a blade or reinforcing canoe keelline.

Static Stroke. A stationary paddle plant, the blade being held in position relative to the canoe.

Static Draw. A stationary high brace with opening powerface, drawing hull or stem to placement.

Static Pry. A stationary high brace, pitched to closing angle of attack and force loaded, moving hull or stem away from paddle.

Stems. The canoe's bow and stern.

Stern. The aft canoe stem.

Stroke. A paddle placement and force loading.

Sweep. An offside turning paddle stroke arcing from bow to stern, or stern to bow (see quarter sweeps).

Symmetry. Shape having front-to-back or side-to-side mirror imagery; hulls, blades, and grips.

Tandem. A canoe designed for two paddlers, or two people paddling one canoe.

Throat. The section of a paddle where shaft and blade join.

Torque. Turning a canoe by introducing rotational force; often inadvertent, as a function of power surges off the centerline.

Torso Rotation. Powering strokes using locked arms and twisting the torso to use the larger back and side muscles.

Track. A canoe's ability to run a straight course.

Traveling Stroke. An old name for C stroke; a solo forward stroke with bow draw and stern pry components.

Trim. Fore to aft canoe leveling or pitching.

Tumblehome. The inward curve of a canoe hull from maximum beam to the rails.

Turning Draw. The combination of static draw, pitched reverse quarter sweep to bow, and a bow draw; duffek.

Wedge. A maneuver, usually outside heeled, where jams or inverted jams deflect the forward stem inside a carved turn.

Weight Shift. Fore/aft movement of paddler trimming hull.

Yaw. The canoe's tendency to turn off course, generally caused by torquing components in strokes, but can be induced by heel.

Colophon

The text of this book was set in a digital version of Goudy Old Style, a typeface created in 1915 by Frederic Goudy for American Type Founders. The subheads are set in Goudy Heavy Face and the captions are set in Goudy Catalogue Italic.

The chapter numbers were created using the Optima typeface. The canoe and paddle drawings were created by Frank Logue, who designed and composed this book for Carolina Graphics group in Rome, Georgia.

Printed and bound by Walsworth Publishing Company in Marceline, Missouri.